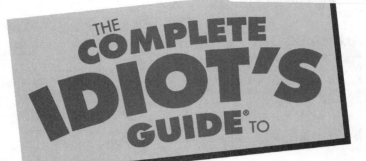

THE COMPLETE IDIOT'S GUIDE® TO

Money
for *Teens*

by Susan Shelly

ALPHA

A member of Penguin Group (USA) Inc.

*This book is dedicated to my very favorite teenager,
Sara Kathryn McGovern. I hope you'll have as much
joy in your life as you've brought into mine.*

ALPHA BOOKS

Published by the Penguin Group

Penguin Group (USA) Inc., 375 Hudson Street, New York, New York 10014, U.S.A.

Penguin Group (Canada), 10 Alcorn Avenue, Toronto, Ontario, Canada M4V 3B2 (a division of Pearson Penguin Canada Inc.)

Penguin Books Ltd, 80 Strand, London WC2R 0RL, England

Penguin Ireland, 25 St Stephen's Green, Dublin 2, Ireland (a division of Penguin Books Ltd)

Penguin Group (Australia), 250 Camberwell Road, Camberwell, Victoria 3124, Australia (a division of Pearson Australia Group Pty Ltd)

Penguin Books India Pvt Ltd, 11 Community Centre, Panchsheel Park, New Delhi—10 017, India

Penguin Group (NZ), cnr Airborne and Rosedale Roads, Albany, Auckland 1310, New Zealand (a division of Pearson New Zealand Ltd)

Penguin Books (South Africa) (Pty) Ltd, 24 Sturdee Avenue, Rosebank, Johannesburg 2196, South Africa

Penguin Books Ltd, Registered Offices: 80 Strand, London WC2R 0RL, England

Note: This publication contains the opinions and ideas of its author. It is intended to provide helpful and informative material on the subject matter covered. It is sold with the understanding that the author and publisher are not engaged in rendering professional services in the book. If the reader requires personal assistance or advice, a competent professional should be consulted.

The author and publisher specifically disclaim any responsibility for any liability, loss, or risk, personal or otherwise, that is incurred as a consequence, directly or indirectly, of the use and application of any of the contents of this book.

Most Alpha books are available at special quantity discounts for bulk purchases for sales promotions, premiums, fund-raising, or educational use. Special books, or book excerpts, can also be created to fit specific needs.

For details, write: Special Markets, Alpha Books, 375 Hudson Street, New York, NY 10014.

Publisher
Marie Butler-Knight

Product Manager
Phil Kitchel

Managing Editor
Jennifer Chisholm

Acquisitions Editor
Randy Ladenheim-Gil

Development Editor
Tom Stevens

Production Editor
Billy Fields

Copy Editor
Rachel Lopez

Illustrator
Jody P. Schaeffer

Cover Designers
Mike Freeland
Kevin Spear

Book Designers
Scott Cook and Amy Adams of DesignLab

Indexer
Brad Herriman

Layout/Proofreading
Angela Calvert
Svetlana Dominguez
John Etchison
Elizabeth Louden

Contents at a Glance

Contents

Introduction

It's increasingly recognized that teenagers and their money are forces to be reckoned with. You, as a collective group of teenagers, wield tremendous buying power, making you very attractive to all kinds of retailers and advertisers. Statistics from the U.S. Department of Labor show that the average teenager spends almost $5,000 a year. That's more than double from just five years ago.

While you're spending more money, you're also becoming smarter about your finances. You're not only stashing money away in savings accounts, you're investing in CDs (certificates of deposit), mutual funds, and the stock market. You're not only buying from other people's businesses, you're starting and running your own businesses.

Teenagers are innovative, creative, and not afraid of the future. However, to ensure a financially comfortable future, you need to know even more about the best ways to handle your money. Your personal finances are important to retailers and marketing firms, but they're even more important to you.

This book walks you through the basic money matters and delves into weightier topics such as credit cards, investing and investment clubs, and being an entrepreneur. You'll learn how to make the most of your money so you'll have more to save, invest, and spend.

What You'll Find in This Book

The Complete Idiot's Guide to Money for Teens is written in six parts:

Part 1, "Money: A Fact of Life," explains why money is so important in our society and the role it plays in most of our lives. You no doubt have discovered the power of money by now. You probably understand that money not only lets you buy what you need and want, it gives you choices and lets you do what you want to do.

This part also discusses the importance of keeping money in perspective. After all, it's important, but it doesn't by itself ensure happiness or contentment.

Part 2, "So, How Are You Gonna Get It?" deals with the big problem that most teens have: There just never seems to be enough money for all the stuff you want to buy and do. Everything is expensive these days, and it's hard to make your allowance or paycheck stretch to cover everything you want or need.

You'll learn how to negotiate for more allowance or to find a job that you can handle while still leaving time for the other parts of your life. You'll also find that your net worth might be more than you think. It's possible that you have some money lying around that you don't even know about!

"Smart Saving" is the title of **Part 3**, and in it you learn to do just that. You'll take a little test to find out whether you're more of a saver or a spender. If you find it easier to spend than to save, don't be discouraged. There are tons of other people with the same problem, and there are ways to curb spending so you can save more.

Regardless of how much you save, however, you should be getting the best deal you can. Interest rates vary dramatically, depending on where you stash your money. And you, of course, want to get the highest interest rate you can.

In **Part 4, "Smart Spending,"** you learn that you can stretch your dollars by buying smart. You also learn why you need a budget (everyone does), and what it should include. By keeping an eye on what and how you spend, you can get a lot more of the things you need without sending yourself to the poorhouse.

In **Part 5, "Keeping Track of What You've Got,"** the major topics are opening and keeping a checking account, using a debit card, and negotiating ATM machines. Using checks is great, and a smart idea in many cases. However, if you don't take the time to record what you spend and to balance your checkbook, you'll soon have a mess on your hands.

Debit cards and ATMs are extremely handy; but again, you need to know what you're doing when using them. You need to be aware of all the fees associated with the use of these things, and understand how they affect your bank accounts.

In **Part 6, "Advanced Money,"** you learn about getting and using credit cards, investing your money, and starting your own business. This part is full of practical, useful information that's sure to be interesting and beneficial.

Extras

In addition to the six parts found in this book, you'll find three types of sidebars. These little bits of information are intended to keep you out of trouble, provide hot tips, and give you interesting tidbits that you might not have heard anyplace else.

Money Matters

These tips will keep you informed and in the know about your money and personal finances.

Imagine That

These statistics and offbeat bits of information are great to pass along to your friends. They'll think you're just so smart!

Scary Stuff

Hopefully, these warnings will keep you from making some common mistakes that could negatively affect your finances.

Acknowledgments

The author would like to thank the many people who provided time, interest, information, and resources for this book, especially the editors at Alpha Books: Randy Ladenheim-Gil, Tom Stevens, Billy Fields, and Rachel Lopez.

A great deal of thanks, as always, goes to Bert Holtje of James Peter Associates, with whom it is a pleasure and a privilege to be associated.

Much appreciation for valuable advice and their shared knowledge is extended to Sarah Young Fisher, George Shoffner, and John Sortino.

As always, the most special thanks goes to Mike, Sara, and Ryan McGovern.

Trademarks

All terms mentioned in this book that are known to be or are suspected of being trademarks or service marks have been appropriately capitalized. Alpha Books and Penguin Group (USA) Inc. cannot attest to the accuracy of this information. Use of a term in this book should not be regarded as affecting the validity of any trademark or service mark.

Part 1

Money: A Fact of Life

Just stop for a minute and think about the role that money plays in your life. Chances are it's pretty darned important. You probably think about and talk about money a lot, because you need it for just about everything.

Without money, life as you know it would come to a quick and abrupt halt. You'd no longer be able to stop on your way home from school for a soda or coffee. You wouldn't get new games for your Nintendo, or that cute sweater from the Gap. Without money, your choices and options become limited. You can't do what you please, or live the way you might like to.

Money is important, and it's a major fact of life in our society. In this part, we explore the role of money in our lives, look at how we treat money, and examine the history of money. We also discuss the limitations of money, and how it's important to keep money in perspective.

Chapter 1

Why Money Is So Important

In This Chapter

✧ Understanding money in our society

✧ Looking at what money means to you

✧ What you buy with the money you have

✧ Considering the cost of living on your own

✧ Taking advantage of the saving years

There's no question that money is important in our society. It's a big deal—a really big deal. It's next to impossible to live without money. Take a look around your room. Chances are you have a phone, a CD player, and maybe a TV. Maybe you've got your own computer or one you share with a sister or brother. You probably have a closet full of clothes and a fridge full of food in the kitchen. All the things we have (and often take for granted) are there because somebody had the money to buy them. We need money to get the necessities of life—and more money for all the extra stuff we want.

Just think for a minute what your life would be like without money. No money equals no cool clothes, no after-school stops at Burger King, and none of those little gizmos and gadgets you like so much. Having no money is a big bummer for you, and an even bigger bummer for adults. If your personal cash flow dries up, you might miss out on tickets for the Blink-182 concert. If your parents' cash flow stops, you all miss out on having a place to live and enough to eat.

You've gotta have it, there's no question about it. Money really does make the world go 'round, and we Americans are known for wanting to grab more than our fair share of it. We guzzle more resources, buy more, use more, and throw more away than any other society on earth. We love money, and we love what we can buy with it. Let's have a look at our society's attitudes toward money and at some of the ways we spend what we make.

Money and the American Way of Life

Americans have great affection for money, and teens are no exception. We love to make it and we love to spend it. We have thousands of stores in which to shop, millions of items available to buy, and an army-load of advertisers telling us that we need it all. Old Navy, Delia's, Nordstrom, and Bloomingdale's; clothes, jewelry, cosmetics, electronics, and music—the lists are endless. So, what are some of the things teenagers die for (at least according to advertisers)? Check out the pages of your favorite teen magazine or the local newspaper sometime, and you'll get a list that looks something like the following:

✧ Designer jeans—can't live without them

✧ That little tube top with the glitter front to go with the jeans

✧ Skin care products by the zillion—everybody knows that acne is the pits!

✧ Hair highlighters—because you're worth it

✧ Cool shoes from Skechers

- ✧ Cool bathing suits from OP
- ✧ Watches that come in seven colors—one for each day!
- ✧ Makeup, nail polish, and more makeup
- ✧ A Gateway desktop computer
- ✧ Jelly Bean phones, CD players, microwaves, TVs, and Nintendos (check out all the colors you can get)
- ✧ A Powerpuff stamp set (better order two!)
- ✧ Bubble gum, candy, soda, and hamburgers

Advertisers would like you to believe that you really can't live without this stuff, and often they succeed. Don't think, though, that only teens are susceptible to hype. Adults fall for the same kinds of advertising ploys all the time—only their toys tend to be bigger and more expensive, such as sport utility vehicles, convertibles, and platinum jewelry.

The point is that most of us like stuff, and we want stuff—lots of it. We like to do things, too. All of this stuff, and these activities that we love, cost money—a lot of money.

The American economy has been booming, and many Americans, though certainly not all, have been thoroughly enjoying the results. Take a drive around the area where you live and check out the brand-new housing developments with the SUVs parked out front. Notice all the fancy, new electronic stuff that keeps getting sleeker and more sophisticated all the time.

Chances are your school's parking lot is filled with cars, and I'm not talking Dad's old junkers, either. How many of your friends have their own cell phones or big-screen TVs in their family rooms?

There's plenty of money out there, and Americans are making it and spending it in record amounts. There are more than 3.5 million millionaires in America today, and more people have money invested in the stock market than ever before.

Money Matters

We hear a lot about the ongoing prosperity in America, but don't be deceived into thinking that the boom has benefited all Americans. The income gap between the poorest and richest U.S. families continues to widen.

Money always has been and continues to be a big deal in our society. It buys us what we need and what we want. In many ways, money defines who we are. Because money is held in such high esteem, people who have it generally are admired and respected, regardless of whether they deserve to be. We assume, often incorrectly, that somebody who has a lot of money must be smart, whereas someone without money is somehow deficient.

This isn't to say that all Americans are obsessed with money and what it can buy for them. There are people—a lot of people—who are satisfied with what they've got and think that they have enough money. In fact, the *USA Weekend*'s 12th annual Teen Survey conducted in 1999 showed that two-thirds of the teens questioned feel they have enough money. On the other hand, more than half of the teens interviewed expect to be better off financially than their parents are when they get to be the same age. So, although they're content with what they've got now, they're not limiting the financial level they hope to attain in 20 or 30 years.

Yep. Money is real important in America, and there are a lot of people who are willing to do whatever it takes to get it. People work for money, fight for money, marry for money, and sometimes kill for it. In this chapter, we look at why money is such a big deal and the role it plays in your life.

Understanding the Role of Money in Your Life

It's not only millions of adults who are enjoying the benefits of the strong economy. Teens, too, are riding the wave of economic prosperity, whether with money they earn themselves or with handouts from Mom and Dad.

Imagine That

Of the nearly 200,000 teens who participated in the *USA Weekend* survey, half of them had spent $20 or more in stores during the week the survey was taken.

Statistics from the U.S. Department of Labor show that, as a group, teenagers spent $141 billion in 1998—an average of $4,548 each. That's up 60 percent from just five years earlier, and translates—even at today's high prices—into a lot of CDs, clothes, jewelry, and burgers.

Because teens have this tremendous buying power, you're prime targets for retailers and advertisers. Magazines geared toward teens are packed with ads for clothing brands, skin care products and makeup, computer stuff, and jewelry—you've seen them. Hollywood loves teens, too, and is more than happy to get its share of your money by producing movies that you're sure to want to see.

Many of you are big spenders, to be sure. On the other hand, *USA Weekend*'s 12th annual Teen Survey, published May 2, 1999, shows that nine out of ten teens are saving money; most with specific goals in mind. The survey states that you know way more about making, saving, and investing money than teens ever have before. A lot of you have your own bank accounts and control your own money. Some of you are buying certificates of deposit or investing your money in mutual funds. You're money smart and, as a group, you're looking ahead.

Imagine That

According to the *USA Weekend* survey, girls save their money mostly for college, whereas boys save to buy cars. Younger teens save, too, but mostly with no specific goals in mind.

"You have to think long term," said Brooke Richey, a 17-year-old *USA Weekend* survey participant from Ridgeley, West Virginia. "I know how expensive college is, and I know you have to go to college if you want to do something important. That's why, instead of going shopping every weekend, I save my money."

Not everyone, however, shares Richey's view. Researchers recently followed 9,000 teens from around the country for two years to determine what they were buying and how much they were spending. One of the teens, Saytoria Mathis, a 17-year-old from Milwaukee, says she spends between $150 and $175 a week on clothes, shoes, CDs, and jewelry, and she doesn't think twice about it. Most of the money is handed to her by her mother and grandmother. Mathis doesn't like to wait to buy something she wants. "I want it when I want it," she says.

Attitudes toward money vary, but the need and desire to have it doesn't. No matter how much you have, how you get it, or what you decide to do with it, money plays and will continue to play an important role in your life.

You Just Can't Live Without It

Maybe you're saving for a car or to help out with college expenses. It might be that you just can't live without the latest Abercrombie & Fitch sweater, or you just like to have enough pocket change to grab a snack when you want one. Regardless of what you use your money for, you've gotta have it.

Imagine That

Although half of the participants in a survey by *Young Money* magazine said they spend less than $25 a month on fast food, 33 percent reported spending between $25 and $50, and 18 percent spend $50 or more. That's a lot of burgers and fries!

Most teenagers depend primarily on their parents for support. I mean, your parents probably don't charge you rent to live in their house, or make you pay for the food you eat. They probably buy your clothes, or at least some of them. If you work and make your own money, you probably use it for extra stuff that you want or to help with your expenses. Maybe you buy your own Nikes or pay for your own car insurance.

No matter where your money comes from, it's a sure bet that you need it to get through the day. It's easy to overlook how much you spend during an ordinary day on things you don't even think about—a soda here, a bus fare there. Little things add up; if you think about it, you might find out that you spend more than you realize. Consider for a minute how easy it is to spend a lot of money on everyday stuff like movies, ATM fees, bottled water, cosmetics, gifts, admission fees, and fast food.

Our world is expensive, that's for sure, and it costs money to participate in much of it. You could get away without spending any money, I guess. It wouldn't be easy, though, and it wouldn't always be a lot of fun. You couldn't go to a movie, or even rent one from the video store. You could go to the mall with your friends, but you couldn't buy a CD, a lipstick, or get anything at the food court. There'd be no new dress or shoes for the holiday dance at school, and you couldn't borrow your parents' car if it needed gas. That's not to say there aren't all kinds of ways to have fun free of charge (we'll have a closer look at that topic in Chapter 3, "Keeping Money in Perspective"), but a lot of the things you like to do come at a price.

Money Matters

Get a friend or two and make a pact that you'll go for a week without spending a dollar. Then see if you can.

Although you need money now, you'll need it even more in a few years. In the next section, we look more closely at the cost of living, at home or on your own. If you think you need cash for the extra stuff you like to buy now, wait until you get a look at how much it would cost to live on your own in the real world!

How Much Money Does One Person Need?

We're going to spend a good part of Chapter 2, "Using Money to Get What You Want," discussing the difference between need and want, so for now just keep in mind that there's a huge difference. Most of us have far more than we really need, and often we confuse our needs with our wants. There are, however, things that we really do need. We need food, clothing (although we don't need a closet stuffed with so many shirts and sweaters that we have a hard time closing the door), a place to live, and a way to get around. When you're living at home, most of your needs are taken care of. When you're on your own, it's really a different story.

Life on Your Own

Most teenagers occasionally think about what it would be like to move out of Mom and Dad's house and get a place of their own. Wouldn't it be great! A little apartment someplace, with nobody to tell you that you've gotta clean up your room or what time you need to be home. You could eat whatever you wanted to, whenever you wanted to. Your friends could hang out forever and nobody would tell them it's time for them to go home.

Maybe life on your own would be great, but it also would be super expensive. Let's have a look at some of the expenses you incur when you're supporting yourself. I'll bet there are some costs you've never even thought about, such as:

✦ **Rent.** Take a couple of minutes and go grab your local newspaper. Turn to the classified ads—the real estate ones, not the personals—and find the section that lists properties for rent. You might read something such as, "Sunny 2nd flr. 1 BR apt. Priv. entrance, washer, dryer, fully equipped kitchen." Sounds good, right? It's everything you need. Then you get to the cost. $610 a month. Oops! Sure, if you look hard enough and you're in a location where cheap rentals are available, you might be able to find something for less than that. On the other hand, if you're in a really desirable area with few rentals available, you might have to pay a lot more.

✦ **Furniture.** Assuming you wouldn't want to live in an empty apartment, you'll need furniture. Maybe a sofa, a

11

couple of chairs, and a coffee table will do for the living room. Oh, you'll probably want a TV, and you'll need a table for that. You'll want a table and chairs for the kitchen or dining room and a bed to sleep in. A nightstand and a dresser to keep your clothing in would be nice, too. If you had to buy all this new, it would cost thousands of dollars. Fortunately, there are a lot of used furniture shops, so you should be able to get everything for $1,000 or so.

Money Matters

Living with only the barest necessities might not sound so bad. It might even seem appealing. Trust me on this one: It would get really old, really fast.

✧ **Phone and cable.** Unless you want to walk down to the corner pay phone every time you need to make a call, you'll need a telephone. You'll find out when you call the phone company that your telephone will cost $40 or $50 to install, and you'll probably need about $100 for a deposit on it. Count on paying $25 or $30 a month for basic phone service (long distance calls are extra). Cable TV is great, but it's expensive. Figure about $50 a month, plus $75 or so to install it.

✧ **Electricity, heat, and water.** If you're lucky these costs might be included in your rent. If not, add them to the cost of living on your own.

✧ **Other stuff.** Sheets and blankets for the bed, towels, a couple of lamps, dishes to eat from, silverware, pots and pans, some glasses, a picture or two for the walls, toilet paper, toothpaste .... You need a lot of stuff, and it all costs money to get.

These are only some of the many costs associated with living on your own. We haven't even talked about food, entertainment, or clothing. Suffice to say it costs a lot—a whole lot—of money to live on your own.

Hanging In at Home

There's a very good reason that most teens live at home and depend on their parents to supply most of what they need. Most teens don't have enough money to support themselves.

The years that you spend at home are prime time for saving money. If you've got a job, or even just get allowance, try to save a little bit of each pay. Even if it's just a couple of dollars, it'll add up. And, saving even a little shows that you're in control of your money and thinking ahead. You'll learn a lot more about saving in Part 3, "Smart Saving."

Although you might be able to save a little, living at home doesn't mean you don't need money to spend. We've already discussed dozens of examples of teen money grabbers, and I'm sure you can think of dozens more. The amount of money you need depends on what you're responsible for buying and how much stuff you want. Justin might be perfectly happy with only $10 a week to spend, whereas Jonathan is sure he can't possibly get along with less than $50.

Katie works after school and buys all her own clothes, make-up, movie tickets, and so forth. Obviously, she needs more money than Jess, whose parents buy all her clothes and everything else. Although the amount of money needed varies from person to person, the need for money applies to everyone. Our society is money oriented and money driven, and you need it to be in the game.

The Least You Need to Know

✧ Money not only buys what you need, it provides security, status, and power.

✧ There are millions of items and activities to spend money on, and advertisers do an effective job of making us want them all.

✧ Teens have tremendous buying power, and are an important group of consumers.

✧ Saving money while you're still living at home can give you a head start for your post–high school years.

✧ The amount of money needed varies from person to person, but everybody needs some.

Chapter 2

Using Money to Get What You Want

In This Chapter

✧ Understanding the power of money

✧ The fuzzy line between want and need

✧ Buying stuff just for fun

✧ When need becomes very clear

✧ Intangible things we get from having money

Everyone who lives independently needs money. There's just no way around it. Even people who don't live entirely independently (such as you) still need money to achieve a level of independence.

When you were a baby, you didn't care at all about money. You didn't even know what it was. You were completely dependent on the adults who cared for you, and you cared only about your most basic needs. When you were a small child, you probably didn't care much about money either; it simply wasn't an issue. Everything you needed was provided for you and your wants were much fewer than they are as a teenager.

Money probably started to become an issue for you at about age seven or eight when you began to realize that money's the stuff that can get you want you want. Your needs at that age were still being taken care of, so you didn't have to think about money as it related to buying food, providing your shoes, or paying the rent or mortgage. You began to focus instead on the non-necessary things that you then understood you could buy if you had money.

It probably was at about this age that you understood the 10-dollar bill your aunt gave you for your birthday could buy you that Ninja Turtle set you'd been scoping out at the toy store, or that tennis outfit, complete with a racket and sneaks, for your favorite Barbie doll.

When that realization occurs, money takes on a new importance and life is never the same. All of the sudden, you sense the power of money. In this chapter, we take a hard look at money and the things it can get you. Some of those things are tangible—you can hold them in your hand or put them in your room. Others are intangible—you can't see them or physically have them but they're just as important.

Buying Stuff You Need—or Think You Need

It's fair to say that most teenagers spend their own money on stuff that they want rather than on stuff they need. This is because most teens have parents or other adults who provide their basic needs for them. Chances are your shelter, food, and at least some of your clothing needs are taken care of for you.

It's a good bet that you don't pay for your own schooling, to see the doctor when you're sick, or for the glasses you need because you're nearsighted. I doubt you footed the bill for the braces you had when you were 10 or 11, or for that dictionary your third-grade teacher recommended that you have to use at home.

I would venture that most teens don't have to worry about most of their needs and probably get a lot of help with their wants, too. There are a lot of costs involved in that period between the time you're 12 and the time you're 20. Expenses such as fees to participate on athletic teams, class trips, birthday presents for friends, recreational activities, CDs and video games, dance lessons, camps, music lessons, and so on, add up fast.

Imagine That

Although many children and teens enjoy the benefits and luxuries of belonging to a middle-class family, there still are more than 12 million children in the United States living in poverty, according to The Children's Defense Fund.

None of these expenses is a real need, although to you they might seem to be. Because your parents probably pay for your basic needs and a lot of your wants, too, you are able to supplement your wants and needs with money of your own.

When basic needs are satisfied, we tend to escalate wants into needs. If you haven't had a meal for three days because you have no money to buy food, you absolutely know that food is a need and the latest Christina Aguilera CD isn't. But, if you get all the food you want every day and you never have to think about being hungry, you're likely to place a great deal more importance on the CD.

Buying Stuff We Don't Need, But Want Anyway

There's nothing wrong with buying things that we want, as long we keep it to a reasonable limit and keep our spending habits in perspective. Sometimes it's fun to go out and buy something you know you don't need, just because you want it. We're extremely fortunate to live in a society where many of us are able to do that from time to time. It feels good sometimes to buy something that you really like, even though you know full well that you could live without it.

Scary Stuff

Beware of the temptation to buy and buy and buy. Too much neat stuff can quickly become a liability when you can no longer move around in your room because of it.

However, if you max out your credit card or run up more than you should on your parent's credit card, or continually spend all the money you have on frivolous items, you're obviously buying too many things that you want. The trick is to balance buying what you need with what you know you don't need, but want anyway.

Our homes are filled with decorative items that we buy strictly because we want them—not because we need them. Look around your own room. How many clothes are in your closet that you bought (or got somebody to buy for you) because you liked them, not because you needed them?

The teenager's room in my own house is filled with glittery lotions, dozens of bottles of nail polish, and a box overflowing with hair accessories. There are scented candles and a glittery star night light. There's a light that rotates when it's turned on, allowing different views of dolphins. There's a CD player, a portable CD player, and CDs spread across a table and the floor. There are at least 100 books on her bookshelf, many of which she's bought for herself.

None of these things are necessary, but they're fun, and they help to make my daughter's room her own space. As long as unnecessary spending doesn't get out of hand or interfere with buying what you really do need, it's okay.

Knowing the Difference Between Want and Need

As stated earlier, the difference between want and need becomes fuzzy when our needs are met and we have money to spend on non-necessities. All of the sudden, you feel as if you really need that black leather jacket, even though you already have two warm coats.

If you think carefully about it, chances are you'll realize that most, if not all of the things you say you need really are things you can live very well without.

Someone once told me that the difference between want and need became very clear to him in the emergency room after he'd been in a serious motorcycle accident. His wants cleared away, he said, completely replaced with a single need—to live. The loss of his motorcycle didn't matter, nor the thought of anything he owned. He needed only to live.

Money Matters

Make a list of everything you think you need at this particular time. Then go over each item and really ask yourself if it's a need or a want. Chances are you'll discover the great majority of items on your lists are wants, not needs.

Hopefully, you have a sense of the difference between need and want and won't have to face adverse circumstances to make the concept clear to you. Remember that many of the things you really need—love, friendship, hope, and a feeling of security—aren't dependent on money.

Money Gets You Stuff You Can't See

You know that money gets you stuff (or allows others to get you stuff) that you really need—your food, medical care, clean water, shelter, and clothing. You also know that money gets you stuff that you don't need, but want anyway. Did you ever stop to think about the things money gets you that you can't see? In our society, money gets you power. It gets you respect. It opens doors that otherwise might remain closed. It gets you independence, enables you to have choices, and sometimes causes a great deal of trouble and heartache. Let's consider some of the nontangible things that money brings.

Scary Stuff

Although many people who have money are deserving of respect, be careful to not assume that respect and money are interchangeable. Look instead for qualities such as honesty, sincerity, integrity, and kindness.

Power and Status

Money is a source of power and status. People who make a lot of money—and have a lot of money to spend—often are considered to be powerful people because of it.

Even kids recognize at an early age that having money to spend provides them with a feeling a power. It allows them to take control of a situation. A lot of money sometimes allows people to control other people as well. Kids learn this feeling of power from adults, whom they observe showing off purchases or talking admirably about their neighbor's new BMW. They quickly associate money with success and power.

The well-respected business magazine, *Forbes*, releases a list each year called *Forbes Top CEOs: Corporate America's Most Powerful People*. As you might imagine, the list is based on how much money each CEO has been able to make during the preceding year.

We think of politicians as being powerful people. Many of them also are wealthy people who have used their money to run campaigns and get elected. Those who don't have money of their own must raise money or get support from their respective political parties.

Not all powerful people are rich; some have been very poor. The power of Rosa Parks, the brave African American woman from Alabama who refused to give up her seat on a bus to a white man, or the power of Mother Theresa, the nun who worked tirelessly to care for the world's poorest and most desperate people, came from courage and conviction. However, these examples, and others like them, are the exceptions. Whether it's right or not, money and power go hand in hand in this country.

Respect

We tend to look up to people who have a lot of money, whether or not their characters warrant it. Young drug dealers on city streets often have said that they enjoy the respect they get from having money and, as a result, power.

People who make or win a lot of money in a short time often recognize a new sense of respect shown toward them. It's not that they've changed or are any more worthy of respect than they were before their financial situations changed. The respect they're seeing comes merely from the fact that they now have money. Of course, many people who don't have a lot of money are very worthy of respect, and enjoy the respect they deserve.

Independence

One of the really good things having money does for you is to allow you independence. It's a great feeling to have enough money to do what you want without having to ask somebody for help.

If you work and earn money, you've probably enjoyed a sense of this feeling of independence. As you get older and make even more money, you'll enjoy the transition you'll make from dependence to independence.

Money Matters

Even young children quickly learn that having a little money of their own makes them more independent. Consider the second grader who, without asking her mother, remembers every Thursday to take 50 cents to school so she can buy ice cream after lunch. She's taken a step toward independence by doing so.

Choices

Another great value of money is that it gives you choices. Consider this: If the salary you get from your minimum-wage job is the only income you have and you have two young children to support, your choices are going to be extremely limited. You won't be able to decide to upgrade your apartment, send your children to a better day-care center, or to take a vacation. Your only choice will be to manage, or to try to find a better job so you'll make more money.

As an adult, having money allows you a great many choices and possibilities. You can consider taking a trip, buying a piano, or moving from your apartment to a home. You can choose to go back to school, switch jobs or careers, or have another child.

As a teenager, your choices are more limited, but having money does provide you with options you might not have without it. Money is necessary to have choices. The freedom that money provides is one of the best things about it.

Money Matters

Having money is a great liberator and can limit worries about the future. For instance, a couple who has $100,000 invested in a sound fund earmarked for their child's college tuition probably has fewer concerns about their financial future than a couple who hasn't saved a dime toward college tuition.

Worries

When you never seem to have enough money, it's hard to imagine that there's a downside to having lots more than you need, but there are actually a lot of downsides. Money can provide a sense of financial security and give you options and choices, but it also can be the source of a lot of headaches.

Even when you just have a moderate amount of money, you need to keep track of it and decide what you'll do with it. You want to make sure it's safe, and hopefully make it work for you to make more money. Most people deal well with these issues because they don't have extraordinarily large amounts of cash. People without much money who have suddenly acquired large amounts, however, often have difficulty adjusting to their change of status and managing their newly found wealth.

Imagine That

According to Jonathan Freedman's book *Happy People*, there's a high proportion of unhappy doctors and lawyers as compared to those in other professions. This is interesting, considering the fact that doctors and lawyers generally make a lot of money compared to many other professions.

Sometimes people who have a lot of money become very suspicious because they think everyone they meet is trying to get a piece of their wealth. Others obsess over their money, never really enjoying it because they're too worried about losing it.

Money has been the downfall of many, many people. There are those who never have enough, so they embezzle from their companies or bilk their clients out of their lives' savings. There are those who get so far in debt they become completely hopeless and end up killing themselves.

When kept in perspective, money is a useful commodity that can bring happiness and comfort to your life. When it becomes overly important, however, it can quickly cease to be a good thing and become a real burden.

What Happens When You Don't Have Enough

Although having money can bring accompanying problems, not having enough money can be an even greater source of trouble. Not having enough money doesn't mean that you won't be able to buy a pair of shoes to go with your new dress for the dance. It doesn't mean having to stay at home for a night while your friends go out to dinner because you spent all your money on a video game. Not having enough money is way more serious than those things.

Try to imagine what it would be like if your family didn't have enough money to pay for oil for the furnace. Think about waking up in a cold house that you know will remain cold all day. Or, picture your little sister being very, very sick, but your parents are unable to take her to the doctor because there is no money to pay.

People who don't have enough money suffer, both in America and around the world. In some countries, virtually everyone is poor. About 40,000 people around the world, most of them children, die every day from hunger or hunger-related diseases. Even in America, nearly 13 percent of people are considered to be living in poverty.

Money Matters

To get an idea of what real poverty is like, go to The Great Depression at www.geocities.com/Athens/Olympus/1545.

Being aware of what some people don't have can help to make you more appreciative of what you do have. And, recognizing the difference between want and need can help you to better manage your money.

The Least You Need to Know

✧ Most teens aren't responsible for their basic needs such as food and shelter, so the money they spend tends to be for things they want but don't actually need.

✧ Buying something just because you want it is okay, as long as it doesn't get out of control.

✧ There's a fine line in the minds of many people between want and need, but the distinction often becomes clear in times of great adversity or emergency.

✧ Money can help us get both tangible items such as clothing and CDs, and intangible things such as independence and respect.

✧ There are many people throughout the world who are miserable because they don't have enough money.

Chapter 3

Keeping Money in Perspective

In This Chapter

✧ Dealing with problems that money causes

✧ Learning to have fun without money

✧ Understanding the relationship between money and happiness

✧ Giving some of what you have

You've read a lot in the last two chapters about how important money is, both to our society and in your own life. There's no question that we need money—and very few people would choose to be without it.

Money buys you stuff you need and stuff you want. It enables us to keep roofs over our heads and to nourish our bodies; and it helps us to enjoy ourselves. It buys designer clothes, cars, and trips to sunny islands. But it doesn't buy you love, and it doesn't—on its own merit—make you happy.

The point of this chapter is to get you to put the matter of money into perspective, help you decide how important it is to you, and help you to decide how important it might be to you later in life.

Money Can't Buy Ya Love

Maybe you've heard that old Beatles song called "Can't Buy Me Love." Whether or not you like the Beatles' music, you'll probably agree that there's some truth to the lyrics of the song, which repeat, "I don't care too much for money, for money can't buy me love."

A lot of people are attracted to money and to people who have money. There are many people, in fact, who are in love with money; but the real kind of love—the kind that makes you happy and makes you feel complete—isn't connected to having tons of money. That love comes from caring deeply for someone, whether it's a boyfriend or girlfriend, a spouse, a parent, a child, or a friend and having that person care for you. It's sharing what's inside you and wanting what's best for the person you love. Those things have little to do with money.

Scary Stuff

Money causes more problems in relationships than almost any other single issue, yet most couples report that they never talk about money until it's become a problem. Not smart!

Not having enough money to be comfortable certainly can create a great strain on a relationship. Couples and families fight about money all the time and money issues are cited as one of the biggest reasons for trouble within marriages. A recent survey by the financial services giant Citibank found that money problems are the leading cause of divorce in this country.

Imagine That

More than one million American households—about one out of every 100—file for personal bankruptcy protection every year. That means the household is not able to pay its debts and files for protection from creditors. Now that's a money problem!

Money problems in families aren't necessarily just between spouses. You've no doubt encountered your fair share of family-related money problems, too. It might seem as if you never have enough money, and your parents either don't help you as much as they could or don't let you spend your money the way you want to. In many cases parents, teens, and money are as volatile a combination as married couples and money.

According to experts, however, money doesn't have to become a major stumbling block in any relationship—marital or family. Consider the following guidelines to help manage money issues within your family:

✧ Be respectful. Agree to talk about money issues reasonably and respectfully. This means no shouting, name calling, or blaming one another for problems.

✧ Decide on a money plan right away to avoid possible problems later. If your parents give you an allowance, for instance, work with them to establish some guidelines about how you'll spend it. Maybe you'll decide that half of what you get is yours to spend however you want and the other half is designated for certain expenses or savings. If you earn your own money, decide with your parents on whether they'll supplement your income, how much you'll spend, how much you'll save, and so forth.

✧ Have a clear understanding of your family's money situation and understand its limitations. If your best friend gets $40 a week plus money for all her clothes and school supplies, it doesn't necessarily figure that you should, too.

✧ Never let money become more important than relationships.

Many people who have lost someone they love say they'd gladly give up all their money to have him or her back. Parents who have endured the agonizing ordeal of having their children kidnapped willingly arrange to have their lives' savings handed over in exchange for getting their child back. Most people who are told they're suffering from terminal diseases and have only a short time to live would be willing to give all the money they have if they could only have their health restored. Money is important, but it really can't buy you love.

Having Fun—Free

What's a teenager to do? It costs $7 or $8 to get into a movie. The $15 it used to take to fill up Mom's gas tank now fills it only two-thirds of the way, thanks to skyrocketing gas prices. A grand latte at Starbucks goes for nearly $3. Soda machines eat up dollar bills and don't give change. The paperback you've been wanting to read might cost you $12.95. Even a burger, Coke, and fries at McDonald's can cost you $5 or more. Just getting through an ordinary day can be super expensive.

On the other hand, it doesn't need to be. Spending lots of money might be more of a habit than a necessity, and there are a lot of ways that you can have fun without spending a lot of money, or any money at all.

Money Matters

Check out www.simpleliving.com for lots of good ideas about having fun without spending a lot of money.

I know a group of five teenagers who get together every Friday or Saturday night for pizza and a video. They meet at one of their houses, have pizza delivered, and watch a video. They always end up having a great time together, and it costs each of them less than $5.

Let's have a look at some other things you can do free or for just a little money, whether on a Friday night, Saturday afternoon, or any other time:

✧ **Get outside.** There are still lots of outdoor activities that won't cost you a penny. Grab some friends and take a hike in a nearby state park. If you're interested in outdoorsy things such as birds or wildlife, these places often offer free nature programs. Find a nearby lake to swim in or head for a friend's pool.

✧ **Check out free stuff going on in your town.** Most communities offer free activities such as concerts or shows. Look up your town or city's Web site or check out the weekend section of your local newspaper to find out what's going on that's free.

✧ **Hang out at the library.** If you haven't visited a public library for a while, you should. Many libraries now offer Internet access, more magazines than you can imagine, videos that you can borrow free, books on tape, and more.

✧ **Work to have fun.** Believe it or not, working together
   with a group can be a lot of fun, and profitable as well.
   Get some friends and some rakes and put the word out
   that you're available for fall clean-up jobs. There are an
   awful lot of aging or busy people around who would
   love to have some reliable, not-too-expensive help.
   You'd have fun and earn some money as well.

You probably can come up with your own ideas for having
free or cheap fun if you put your mind to it. Often, imagina-
tion is more important than money when it comes to entertainment or amusement.

Can Money Really Make You Happy?

Many people think that if they only had more money, they'd
be better off and happier than they already are. "If I only had
$20 more a week, I'd be so much happier," one person might
say; or, "If I only made $300,000 a year instead of $200,000,
I know I'd be a lot happier." You probably can figure that if
Jack's not happy with $200,000 a year, he's probably not
going to be happy with $300,000 either.

Studies have shown again and again that people who have
the material necessities of life—clean water, shelter, breath-
able air, enough food, and adequate clothing—are happier
than those who don't. Once those needs have been met,
however, people with more are not necessarily any happier.

Dr. David Myers, a psychology professor at Hope College in
Michigan and the author of *The Pursuit of Happiness: Who Is
Happy—And Why,* says that people mistakenly think the only
way to be rich is to have great financial wealth. If financial
wealth is your goal and you don't have it, chances are you
won't be happy because you'll feel that you've failed. If you
think about and appreciate what you've got and consciously
try to stop wanting more and more, you'll have a greater
chance at achieving happiness, Myers says.

If you think about it a little, you'll probably realize that
Myers is right. If you "need" the latest style of Nikes even

though they cost $125, refuse to wear anything but Tommy or Nautica, and sneer at anybody who drives a car that's more than two years old, you're setting yourself up for big problems—unless you have access to lots and lots of money.

If, on the other hand, you think the $40 sneaks you get on sale are just fine, you like the way you look in nondesigner jeans and tees, and you think any car is cool as long as it gets you where you need to go, you're probably a pretty happy person. Someone with fewer needs who can enjoy what he or she has without always wanting more is almost sure to be happier than someone who lives in a constant state of "gotta have, gotta get."

Scary Stuff

Since 1960, the rate of violent crime has quintupled in the United States. The divorce rate has doubled and the teen suicide rate has tripled. We have soaring rates of depression. As a country, we're wealthier. But happier? It doesn't seem so.

Income and Happiness

Look at the following chart showing data from a survey conducted by the University of Chicago's National Opinion Center. It divides the nation's population into six groups and shows what percentage of each group is happy and what percentage is unhappy.

What do all those numbers mean? According to the University of Chicago's findings, people who don't have much money ($15,000 might sound like a lot, but it isn't if it's all you've got to live on) are more likely to be unhappy than those earning more. However, it also shows that people who earn more than $75,000 a year aren't much happier than those who earn between $25,000 and $35,000. This seems to support research showing that once basic needs are met, additional money doesn't guarantee additional happiness—or any happiness at all, for that matter. Of course, you usually can find research to contradict research, and surveys and research supporting this topic are no exception.

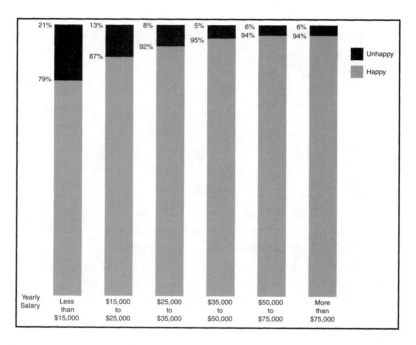

Less Is More?

Joe Dominguez and Vicki Robin, the authors of *Your Money or Your Life,* surveyed more than 1,000 people from the United States and Canada when researching for their book. They asked each person to rank him- or herself on a scale of one to five, with one being "miserable," three being "can't complain," and five being "joyous."

The authors found no correlation between income and happiness. In their survey, in fact, those who earned less than

$1,000 a month reported being slightly happier than those who earned more than $4,000. This is in contrast to the University of Chicago's numbers, which claims that more people of very limited means are unhappier than those of wealth. Go figure.

Scary Stuff

Many people—especially those just entering the workforce—are willing to take jobs they hate if the jobs pay well. When you consider that a job consumes at least one-third of your weekdays, that's an awful lot of life to waste for a good salary.

One thing we do know is that, as a country, we're no happier now than we were 40 or 45 years ago, despite great increases of possessions. The number of people who consider themselves to be "very happy" has leveled off or declined since 1957. This is despite the fact that we consume nearly twice as much in resources today than we did then, when the average size of a house was much, much smaller, and hardly any families had more than one car.

Let's try to put this money and happiness thing in perspective. We live in a country of great wealth. To somebody living in India, for instance, $15,000 a year would be a tremendous amount of money. Americans tend to have a different view on money and possessions because we have so much more than almost everybody else in the world. Quite frankly, we're spoiled. The purpose of this book, however, is not to make you feel guilty because of what you've got or to lecture you on learning to think globally. If you can learn to appreciate what you've got, manage your money well, and try to avoid constantly wanting more and more, there's a really good chance that you'll be happy and contented.

Imagine That

Two-thirds of all the people in the world have a standard of living that's just 20 percent of the U.S. average. That means that the average American is five times better off financially than two out of every three people in the world.

Money and Social Responsibility

To some people, money and social responsibility go hand in hand. To others, the two things are completely unrelated. There are a lot of definitions of social responsibility and a lot of people and groups who have bought into the concept. The Internet is loaded with groups who link themselves with social responsibility.

So, why are all these groups anxious to be known as socially responsible? Because it's trendy, or because they realize it's what we need to do to sustain our society and help the rest of the world? No doubt, each of these groups and the numerous other ones that claim to be socially responsible have their own agendas and their own ideas of what social responsibility means.

Personally, I think that social responsibility is understanding your place in the world, doing what you can to help sustain others, and respecting and protecting your environment.

This doesn't mean that you need to give ten percent of whatever money you have to a charity or that you shouldn't drive or ride in a car. Being socially responsible doesn't mean you need to join a group of monks and sleep on a hard bed for the rest of your life or that you should dispose of all your belongings. It simply means being aware of and appreciating what we have and helping others when we can.

People of great wealth are pressured to be socially responsible and share what they have. Computer guru Bill Gates and his wife founded the Bill and Melinda Gates Foundation and endowed it with more than 17 billion dollars to support philanthropic efforts in the areas of global health and learning. At the beginning of 2000, the foundation had committed nearly $700 million to various agencies.

Of course, Bill Gates's net worth is estimated at more than 80 billion dollars, so what's a few hundred million here and there? The point, though, is that if you have, you might want to consider giving at least a small part of what you have to those who don't.

Helping Out Who You Know

Take a look around your community and you're almost sure to find people who have less than you do. If you're inclined to do so, there's probably a place not far from you that would be happy to have your help. It might be a homeless shelter, or a soup kitchen, or a place where people who don't have much money can buy used clothes and furniture. You don't have to give money in order to help out and be socially responsible. A few hours of your time or donations of clothing or other items you no longer use count, too.

Giving to People You'll Never See

My daughter and I recently participated in a Crop Walk, an event sponsored by Church World Service. We walked five miles to raise money for people who aren't as fortunate as we are. We got sponsors to pay us for each mile we walked, contributed some money ourselves, and trekked along, knowing that most of the money we raised would go to people we would never know or see. We don't know where the money we raised will be used, or who will get it. All we know is that in a small way we were able to help someone who has less than we do.

Many, many people practice social responsibility in small ways all the time. Those with great wealth are able to impact many people when they decide to share what they have. All of us, however, regardless of how much money we have, probably can think of some way to help out someone who has less. Trying to keep money and its importance in a reasonable perspective will help to better appreciate and enjoy what you have, while helping you to remember what others might not have.

The Least You Need to Know

◈ Money-related problems are among the most common that crop up between married couples and in families.

◈ With a little creativity and ingenuity, you can learn to have a lot of fun without spending much money.

◈ Opinions vary, but most research indicates there's no clear link between having a lot of money and being happy.

◈ Social responsibility is caring for the world you live in and the people with whom you share it.

◈ You don't need to have a lot of money to be able to share a bit with those who are less fortunate.

Part 2

So, How Are You Gonna Get It?

No matter how much money you have, it never seems to be enough. You can almost always think of something you'd get, or something you'd do, if only you had the money.

Well, there are ways to earn more money than you might be making now. You might be able to strike a deal to increase your allowance, even if it means some extra chores at home. Maybe it's time to think about getting a job, or a job that pays more than the one you have.

In this part, we look at ways to get money, how to find a decent job, and how to juggle a job with the rest of your life. You'll also learn to figure out your net worth and to locate money you might not even know you have.

Chapter 4

Allowance Only Goes So Far

In This Chapter

✧ Needing money for everything

✧ Understanding the philosophies of allowance

✧ Learning from your allowance

✧ Determining how much allowance is enough

✧ Negotiating for more allowance

You know you need money. The question is how are you gonna get it? We established in the last section that money indeed is a fact of life in our society. Opinions vary on how much you need and what you should do with it, but nearly everyone agrees that money is important—right up there with education, safe communities, and having your hair look good when you go out Saturday night.

It seems to many teenagers that they never have enough money. If this feeling pertains to you, don't be upset. You have lots of company—teens and adults alike. We all are subjected to a lot of pressure from companies that want us to buy their stuff; they can be pretty effective in convincing us that we need all kinds of things.

Believe it or not, teenagers have a lot more spending money today than they ever did before. The problem is there's so much more available to buy. 20 or 30 years ago, teenagers didn't hang out at malls because there were hardly any malls around—and there was no Internet with thousands and thousands of cool things for sale. Today you can walk around the mall and see hundreds of items you'd like to have, all under one roof. You can find almost anything you can imagine on the Internet, and it's all for sale.

When you consider the vast quantity of stuff available to buy compared to the amount of money you have to spend, it's natural that your financial situation seems dismal. In this part of the book we're going to talk about different ways to get some money. Although many teenagers get allowance, most don't get as much as they'd like to, which is why so many teens have part-time jobs. In this chapter, however, we focus on the money you get at home.

Imagine That

Rand Youth Polls showed that teens between 13 and 15 averaged $32 a week in allowance in 1999; teens between 16 and 19 averaged slightly more than $40.

Philosophies of Allowance

It seems that everyone you talk to has a different opinion concerning allowance. Some families and financial advisors believe strongly that it's important for kids and teens to receive regular allowances. Others feel it's better to just hand over money when it's needed. Many people think that allowance should be tied in with chores. Others say that doing chores is part of belonging to a family—not something for which family members should be paid.

Imagine That

Research shows that kids and teens in the Midwest average twice as much allowance as those in the South. This discrepancy could be caused by regional income differences.

Whereas adults have many strong opinions concerning allowance, some informal research on my part reveals that most teenagers have but two:

✧ Allowance is good.

✧ They should get more than they do.

Let's take a look at some of the common philosophies concerning allowance and why people feel the way they do about it. Understanding these different attitudes might help you get a better handle on why your parents do what they do concerning allowance. It also will make you more knowledgeable in case you want to talk to your folks about your allowance.

Earning Allowance for Chores

Giving money for chores done around the house is the most traditional form of allowance. Although it's a common practice used in many homes, it's fallen out of favor among many financial advisors and family counselors.

Some people feel that kids and teenagers should help around the house because they're members of a family and all family members should happily contribute to the upkeep of the home without expecting to be paid for it. After all, they say, does a mother get paid for doing the family's laundry or scrubbing out the toilets a couple of times a week? Does a father get paid for sweeping out the fireplace, fertilizing the lawn, and taking out the trash every Monday and Thursday nights? I don't think so.

These no-allowance-for-chores advocates say teenagers should not get paid for making their beds; setting the table; folding and putting away laundry; keeping their shoes, books, empty soda cans, and underwear off of their bedroom floors; and so forth. They should do these chores willingly, happily, and without complaining, simply because they're delighted to be a part of the family.

Yeah, right. I'm pretty sure there's never been a time when teenagers whistled cheerfully as they emptied trash cans or smiled brightly as they mopped up the kitchen floor, thinking all the while how nice it is to be a member of a family. It sure didn't happen when I was a teenager, and I see no sign of it happening in my own house.

In a perfect world, we all would be happy to do household chores. We'd appreciate the fact that we have toilets to clean, water to use to mop the floor, and the health to complete these tasks. Human nature being what it is, however, most of us don't include chores on our lists of fun things we like to do when we have time.

I say if parents can wrangle chores out of teenagers with an allowance, go for it. After all, somebody's got to empty the trash cans.

Giving Allowance Just Because

Another theory of allowance is to just give it with no strings attached. Teens who get allowance in this form aren't really earning it; they're just getting it.

Most parents, of course, expect their kids to be decent human beings. They expect that they won't look out the window on a Saturday night and see a police officer escorting their son or daughter to the front door, or get frequent calls about outrageous behavior from school principals. Even no-strings-attached allowance could be in jeopardy if those sorts of things occur.

Scary Stuff

Experts warn that parents who give kids big allowances with no expectations attached are passing out unrealistic expectations along with the money. Teens need to know that it takes hard work to earn money. If not, they'll be in for a big surprise later in life.

There are many critics of the no-strings allowance philosophy, but most parents who advocate it say they end up giving their kids money one way or another, so it might as well be in the form of an allowance. If you're going to pass out $20 bills every other day for clothing and other items, why not just give a kid $80 at the beginning of the week and let him or her deal with it?

Using Allowance to Teach About Finances

Using allowance to teach kids and teens how to manage their money is increasingly popular. The practice is applauded by many financial advisors who say it's never too early to begin lessons in personal finances.

Parents sometimes set guidelines for the money they give. An example of such guidelines might be …

- ✧ Sixty percent of the allowance is spending money
- ✧ Thirty percent goes into a savings account
- ✧ Ten percent goes to good deeds

For instance, if Rob gets $50 a week, he could spend $30, put $15 into savings, and give $5 to some good cause such as an offering at church or synagogue or a local charity.

Each family has different ideas about how money should be used, of course, so the guidelines will vary greatly. A family that's deeply committed to helping others might require that 30 or 40 percent of the allowance go to charitable causes. Another family that's not tuned in to charitable efforts might not require that any money be given away.

The $30 that Rob has to spend becomes the crux of the financial management lesson. Out of that $30, he's expected to pay for certain things. Of course, that list also will vary from family to family. Some parents might expect Rob to pay for his own lunches, snacks, movies, and even school supplies. Others figure that $30 probably is enough only for after-school snacks and incidentals at the mall.

Money Matters

Some families reward teens for thriftiness. For example, if lunch at school costs $2.50 but you brown bag it from home, you get to keep the $2.50 to spend on something else.

Experts say parents should follow some rules to successfully use allowance to teach kids and teens about personal finances. They include the following:

✧ Spending guidelines must be clear. If parents expect that 10 percent of the allowance will go to charity and 30 percent to savings, they need to make those expectations clear.

✧ Clearly state what expenses the teenager is expected to pay for out of the allowance. Clothes? Lunches? Or just fun stuff?

✧ Establish that parents still have control over what teens buy. For instance, parents who don't want their kids buying CDs that contain offensive language and topics should specify that those types of purchases aren't permitted.

✧ Pay the same amount at the same time each week, or at whatever interval of time you've agreed on.

✧ No bail-outs allowed. If Rob spends $30 on a new Game Boy game and doesn't save any money to go to the movies with his friends on Friday night, that's his problem.

✧ Give opportunities for earning extra money: extra chores around the house, babysitting, and so forth.

Giving allowance for chores, just giving it with no strings attached, and giving allowance as a means of teaching money management are the three most common philosophies regarding pay for teens. Some families, however, don't believe in allowance at all.

No Allowance

Some families don't give any allowance, either because they can't afford to or they don't think it's the right thing to do. A parent who responded anonymously to an online parents' network sponsored by the University of California at Berkeley had this to say about allowance: "I don't like giving an allowance. I prefer to have more control over the money and provide it for a chosen outfit or activity." Another parent wrote, "I think no allowance is best. I give my kids money only if I feel okay about what they want to buy. If they want to choose what to spend money on, they have to earn it themselves."

Money Matters

If you don't get allowance and would like to, ask your parents to sit down and talk about it. List the reasons you feel you should get allowance, present your ideas, and then listen to your parents' response. They might be pleasantly surprised by your maturity, and you by their decision.

As you've no doubt figured out, the question of allowance is a family matter and must be decided within the family. Some families try them all before they find one that works for them.

How Much Allowance Should You Get?

You probably think the amount of allowance you should get can be summed up in one word: more. Many financial advisors suggest $1 for each year of life. So, you might get $16 a week, whereas your little brother gets $12. That doesn't sound like very much, especially if you compare it with the figures from the Rand Youth Poll: $32 for teens between the ages of 13 and 15 and slightly more than $40 for those between 16 and 19.

Bargaining to Increase Your Allowance

What should you do if you get allowance but the money doesn't begin to pay for all the stuff you need? First of all, know that many other teenagers feel the same way you do. We all know it's a lot easier to spend money than it is to earn it—and everything seems to be costing more all the time.

If you think you need more allowance, take a minute to evaluate the situation. Do your parents normally increase your allowance every year? If so, and the current year is nearly over, you might just want to wait it out until you get your raise.

Money Matters

If you want to ask your parents about increasing your allowance, look for an opportunity when you all have time to sit down and discuss the matter. Everyone is likely to end up feeling frustrated if you have to rush through the discussion.

Has your family's financial situation changed recently? If your dad lost his job three weeks ago, now probably is a really bad time to ask for more allowance. The time also might not be right if your parents just bought a new car or have broken ground for a new home.

However, if everything seems to be status quo and you're not due for a raise soon, go ahead and ask for an increase. Remember, though, as with any time you ask for more pay, there are some guidelines you should follow.

Negotiating 101

There are entire books written on how to negotiate for a raise, much of which doesn't apply to asking good old Mom and Dad for an increase in your allowance. However, some suggestions for negotiating might be of value when you get around to requesting an increase:

✧ Prepare a list of your assets. Write down what you've done well lately, such as all A's on your last report card or walking the dog every day for six weeks.

Money Matters

For tips on negotiating a good raise, check out Hard@ Work's Web site at www.hardatwork.com.

✧ List any ways that you've cut back on spending, especially as it pertains to household expenses. Have you made a special effort to turn off lights when you leave the house? Cut back on the amount of water you use? This shows your parents that you're working to be responsible.

✧ Offer to take on new responsibilities. Maybe you could begin cutting the lawn or handling the laundry.

✧ Compile a list that will show your parents how you spend your money. They might not have a clear idea of what you buy or how much those things cost. For instance, if your mom hasn't bought a soda from a machine for 15 years she might still be thinking that you can get a Coke for 35¢ instead of $1.

✧ Remain calm and in control, even if the discussion isn't going the way you'd like it to. You're not going to make any points by losing your temper or acting like a brat.

✧ Have an idea of how much allowance your friends get and what they do, if anything, to earn it. Your parents might not realize that most of your friends are getting

$10 a week more than you are. Remember, though, that every family has different financial circumstances.

✧ Don't be demanding or threatening when you ask for more allowance. For instance, don't say that if your allowance isn't increased from $10 to $20 immediately, you'll stop doing any chores and never speak to your folks again.

✧ If a brother or sister got an allowance increase recently, ask that sibling how he or she negotiated for the raise.

✧ Catch your parents when they're in a good mood. Experts say people are much more likely to give when they're happy and feeling good about themselves.

Your parents are sure to be impressed if you present your argument for more allowance in an organized and mature manner. They might be so pleased that they'll give you a bigger raise than you'd hoped for.

Scary Stuff

If you lose your temper or go into a sulk when your parents say no to an allowance increase, you might have to wait a long, long time before they're willing to consider the matter again.

Know When to Quit

If you've been asking for more allowance for three months and you haven't seen a penny more, it might be time to forget about it for a while. Perhaps there are circumstances your parents aren't telling you about that would make it difficult for you to get more allowance at this time. Maybe things are shaky at your dad's work and he's unsure about his future there. Many parents won't share that sort of information with their teenagers because they don't want to worry you.

Take what you can get for now, and wait a couple of months to begin another bout of negotiations.

Although it might not be as much as you'd like, allowance is probably the easiest money you receive.

The Least You Need to Know

✧ Teens get and spend more money today than ever before.

✧ Different people have different philosophies concerning allowance.

✧ Experts say an allowance can be a valuable tool in helping teens learn about financial management.

✧ There are varying opinions about how much allowance is appropriate, but many experts recommend $1 for each year of age.

✧ If you're going to ask for more allowance, you should pay attention to how you handle the negotiations.

Chapter 5

Beyond Allowance

In This Chapter

✧ Knowing when it's time to get a job

✧ Finding a job that's age appropriate

✧ Understanding wages and taxes

✧ Fitting work into your schedule

✧ Using a job for more than a paycheck

✧ Getting creative when it comes to jobs

For many teens, there comes a time when allowance just doesn't cut it anymore. The $10 or $15 you get every week doesn't begin to cover your expenses and you're sick and tired of always going to your folks to ask for money. This stage arrives at different times for different people, but you'll know it when you get there. You'll feel more and more uncomfortable asking for money every time you want to go someplace or buy something. You'll strongly wish that you were more financially independent and you'll spend significant amounts of time trying to figure out how to achieve that independence.

For most teens who arrive at this point, the answer is to get a job. Some of you will be excited by the thought of working; others will consider the prospect to be a major bore. If you're in the latter category, read on. Once you consider all the possibilities for different kinds of jobs, you might stop thinking of work as boring and start looking at it as a good opportunity. Remember that not all jobs involve stocking shelves or flipping burgers; with the right attitude, even those that do can be starting points toward something bigger and better.

Is It Time to Look for a Job?

So, how do you know when it's time to look for a job? The following are a few signs that it's time to start filling out applications:

- ✧ You never have enough money to do what you want to do or buy what you want to buy.
- ✧ You feel as if you're constantly asking for money.
- ✧ You've got time on your hands and frequently feel bored.
- ✧ You're looking for a new experience.
- ✧ You think it would be fun to meet some new people.
- ✧ You've decided to start saving money toward a particular goal such as buying a car.

If some of these statements apply to you, you might want to think about job hunting.

Different Jobs at Different Ages

Federal and state laws limit the age at which teenagers can begin working at particular jobs. For instance, you might be able to work at Dairy Queen when you're 14 or 15 but have to wait until you're 16 or 17 to get a job in a manufacturing facility. Under the Fair Labor Standards Act (FLSA) there are certain jobs that are prohibited for all youth under the age of 18. They are …

✧ Any type of mining

✧ Manufacturing or storing explosives

✧ Logging and saw milling

✧ Operating power-driven hoisting equipment

✧ Driving a motor vehicle or being a helper on a motor vehicle

✧ Any job with exposure to radioactive substances

✧ Operating power-driven woodworking machines

✧ Operating power-driving metal forming, shearing, or punching machines

✧ Slaughtering, meat packing, or meat processing

✧ Operating power-driven bakery machines

✧ Operating power-driven paper products machines

✧ Manufacturing brick, tile, and related products

✧ Excavating

✧ Roofing

✧ Wrecking or demolition

✧ Operating power-driven circular saws, band saws, and guillotine shears

Many states also restrict the age at which employees are allowed to serve alcoholic beverages, so if you're looking for a job as a server in a restaurant that has liquor, you might have to rethink your plans.

The FLSA also regulates the specific times and number of hours that teenagers can work. States might have additional restrictions, which will vary from state to state. Most employers are familiar with the laws of their respective states. If you have questions you can check with the U.S. Department of Labor. Check your phone directory for regional numbers.

Scary Stuff

Beware of employers who don't comply with federal or state laws concerning work hours and conditions for teenagers. If you think you might be working for someone like this, you can contact the U.S. Department of Labor.

Minimum Wage and Salary Scales

The federal minimum wage currently is $5.15 per hour, with legislation pending to raise the hourly rate to $6.15 over two or three years. Just because the federal rate is $5.15, however, doesn't necessarily mean that you'll start out earning that amount. The federal rate serves as a guideline, which most states have adopted. Some states, however, set minimum wage rates that are higher than the federal rate; others set lower rates. Seven states: Alabama, Arizona, Florida, Lousiana, Mississippi, South Carolina, and Tennessee have no laws concerning minimum wage..

Imagine That

The first minimum wage of 25¢ per hour was passed in 1938, mostly affecting jobs in manufacturing, mining, and transportation. Unskilled retail and service workers weren't covered by the law.

To find out your state's minimum wage, go to the U.S. Department of Labor's Web site at www.dol.gov/dol/esa/ public/minwage/america.htm.

Imagine That

Fifty-nine percent of all American minimum wage workers are women. Fifteen percent are African American, and 17 percent are Hispanic. More than 10 percent of the entire American workforce lives on minimum wage.

Minimum wage has long been a source of controversy in this country. Some people think it's unfair and that employers should be able to set the wages they'll pay employees. Others feel that minimum wage increases cause workers to lose jobs. Many people support a minimum wage, saying that all workers should be paid enough to make a decent living. Although nearly 12 million workers live on minimum wage, don't assume that it's easy to do so, especially with dependents.

If you get a job at a fast-food place or as a dishwasher in a restaurant, chances are you'll be offered minimum wage. Keep in mind, though, that today's healthy economy and low unemployment rate has prompted many places to increase their starting wages to attract employees from the small pool of available workers.

Before you start a job, be sure to find out from your prospective employer about salary scales. You'll want to find out how and when raises are given. Are they based on job performance or do all employees get raises after they've been on the job for a particular amount of time? Do all employees get the same raises? Can you count on raises at regular intervals?

Don't hesitate to find out what your opportunities are before you agree to take the job. You're perfectly within your rights to ask all the questions you want as long as you do so politely and respectfully.

Those Pesky Things Called Taxes

I've yet to meet a person who likes paying taxes. Unfortunately, they become a part of life as soon as you start making money—and they never go away after that. As you get older and make more money, you'll need to think about things such as deductions and tax shelters.

Money Matters

If you have a job from which you earn a substantial income, ask a parent or friend with some financial knowledge about the possibility of getting your own Individual Retirement Account (IRA). Starting an IRA when you're a teenager could make your life a lot more pleasant when retirement rolls around.

For now, however, there probably are only a few tax-related matters that you need to know about. If you earn less than $4,400 in a year, you don't have to pay federal income tax. That's the good news. If you earn that much or more (up to $23,350), you'll have to hand over 15 percent to good old Uncle Sam. If you earn more than $23,350, you'll pay 28 percent on everything over that amount.

The bad news is that in some states you'll have to pay state income tax, regardless of how much money you make; and

Social Security and Medicare taxes will be deducted from your paycheck. It's a bummer, but you might as well get used to it.

Not All Jobs Are Created Equal

When you think about getting a job, you probably have at least an idea of the kind of work you want to do. Maybe you'd like to work in that cool clothing store in the mall or be a checkout person at the grocery store. If you enjoy working with food, you might think about a job at your local farmer's market or deli. Maybe you think you'd enjoy a telephone sales position or working in a jewelry store. There are many places that hire part-time workers, so there are lots of different opportunities. Keep in mind, however, that not all jobs are created equal.

Scary Stuff

The National Consumers League estimates that every year in the United States an estimated 200,000 youth are injured while working, and 100 are killed.

You read a bit earlier in this chapter that there are certain jobs in which minors aren't permitted to work. The National Consumers League (NCL), a Washington, D.C.–based consumers group, took that list a step further and named the five worst jobs for teenagers. They are …

✧ Delivery and other driving, including operating or riding on forklifts and other motorized equipment

✧ Working alone in cash-based businesses such as fast-food places, convenience stores, and gas stations

✧ Construction, including work in heights and contact with electrical power

✧ Traveling youth crews such as those that sell candy, magazine subscriptions, books, and so forth in strange neighborhoods or different cities and states

✧ Jobs in which employers pay "under the table"

These jobs, the NCL says, have proven time and time again to be dangerous. Even if the job you get is safe and everything about it above board, you may or may not be crazy about it.

Physical Labor

If you're in reasonably good shape and you don't mind giving your muscles a workout, a job requiring physical labor might be a good choice for you. These jobs often involve working outdoors, which appeals to lots of people. You could end up mowing grass at your community swimming pool, where you could chat with friends and cool off during your breaks. Of course, you also could end up in a warehouse someplace, lifting heavy boxes and counting widgets. As I said, not all jobs are created equal.

Money Matters

It's a good idea to talk to people already working in the job that interests you before you decide to take it. You might find out it's a great job—or find out it's not for you.

Using Your Head

If physical work isn't your thing, you'll do better with a different kind of job. If you like working with people, sales might be a good possibility to explore. If you have trouble tearing yourself away from your computer, check the classifieds for jobs that involve inputting information or other computer-related tasks.

Take This Job and Shove It!

If you find yourself working in the job from hell, seriously evaluate the situation. If it's boring, try to think of ways to make it more interesting. Be creative. Ask your boss if there are other jobs you could do. If you feel in any way threatened or unsafe in the job, get out of it immediately.

As long as a job doesn't present a risk, you should try to stick with it if you can. It doesn't look good to other prospective employers if you've had three jobs in the past four months.

Juggling a Job and the Rest of Your Life

If you're like many teenagers today, you're incredibly busy. You're in sports. You have to spend a couple of hours a night doing homework. You have family commitments, and there's never enough time to be with your friends. You play in the marching band and spend every Saturday night from September through November at competitions. You have activities at your church or synagogue. You help your parents take care of your little brother and sister. You visit your grandmother. You try to find time to go snowboarding. You love to read, or ski, or ride your mountain bike.

So, how are you supposed to fit in a job with all the rest of your activities? Good question. Fortunately, teenagers generally have high energy levels (except for in the mornings), and can withstand huge amounts of activity. If you do get a job, you'll have to learn to prioritize. That means doing what absolutely has to be done first, and leaving optional activities for later. Working also will require better organizational and time management skills.

If you decide to get a job, you should make up your mind that you'll be committed to it. It needs to be a priority. You'll need to keep track of the hours you're scheduled to be at work and make sure you have a way to get there and back. By agreeing to work, you're obligating yourself to your employer, just as he or she is obligated to pay you for your services. Before you start filing applications, talk with your parents or guardians about the responsibilities of working and how it will affect not only your life, but your family's life as well.

Imagine That

A study conducted by researchers at the University of Michigan in Ann Arbor revealed that one-third of American teenagers say they feel stressed out on a daily basis. Researchers say it's because teens are increasingly pulled in so many directions, and expectations of them keep getting higher and higher.

There's More to a Job Than the Money You Earn

Most teenagers who get a job do so to make money. Many give little thought past their next paycheck. Every job, however, can be a valuable learning experience (if you choose to learn from it) and you might end up taking more from a job than you ever imagined.

Experience

Every job offers some kind of experience. For instance, if you work at your uncle's restaurant, and you pay attention and ask questions, you might learn more about food service and business than you ever thought you'd know. You could learn how your uncle knows how much of different kinds of food to order, who the suppliers are, and how they get the produce, meats, and breads that end up on the tables. If you work at the clothing store in the mall, you can learn how inventory is ordered, how it's tracked, and where the clothing you sell is made.

Contacts

You've no doubt heard the old saying, "It's not what you know, but who you know." I don't buy into that completely, but there's certainly an element of truth in it. You can never know too many people who are willing to help you, and it's important to remember that most people love to help somebody who's been an enthusiastic, pleasant, hardworking employee.

There are many, many people involved with businesses in your community, some of whom will be able to help you later in life if they're inclined to do so. Maybe you'll need a letter of recommendation for another job, or a reference or two when you start applying for college. Being a great employee, or at least the very best employee you can, ensures that they'll be willing to give you a hand when you need it.

Creative Ways of Making Money

There are as many jobs as there are people to create them. If a "traditional" teenage job such as flipping burgers, stocking shelves, or scooping ice cream doesn't appeal to you, think of something else to do. If you need to have more flexibility with your time than a regular job can offer, consider a different job. There are tons of ways to make money. Get creative and go for it!

Some ideas to consider include cooking or house cleaning, yard work, pet sitting, tutoring, or giving music lessons.

Getting your first job, whether you do something on your own or work for a company, is a big step. Don't be afraid to ask for advice from adults and other teens who already have jobs. If you're dependable, honest, hardworking, and willing to learn, you'll do just fine.

Money Matters

Remember that if you earn more than $4,400 in a year, even if you're on your own, you need to file a tax return for federal income tax.

The Least You Need to Know

✧ When allowance is no longer enough, it might be time to consider getting a job.

✧ The Fair Labor Standards Act prohibits anyone under 18 years old from working in certain types of jobs.

✧ Minimum wage is established by the federal government, but can vary from state to state, depending on state law.

✧ You'll need to pay federal income tax if you earn more than $4,400 a year.

✧ Different people prefer one job to another, depending on their abilities and likes and dislikes.

Chapter 6

Money You Might Already Have

In This Chapter

✧ Considering the possibility of unknown money

✧ Understanding assets and liabilities

✧ Figuring out your net worth

✧ Looking ahead to possible sources of money

Some people keep track of all the money they have, right down to the last penny. They can tell you exactly how many dollars they have invested in various accounts, detail their checking and savings account totals, and tell you how much interest they earned in the past quarter or year. For these kinds of people, there are few financial surprises. Others aren't quite so careful about their money.

Occasionally, there'll be a story in the newspaper or on TV about some guy who just found out he has half a million in a bank account he'd forgotten even existed or a woman who discovers $100,000 in $50 and $100 bills stashed in a shoebox that her husband kept in his clothes closet until he died. Although something that drastic won't ever happen to most of us, it might be that you're not exactly sure of how much money you have and where it is.

If that's the case, it's perfectly understandable. Parents, grand-parents, other relatives, and friends sometimes open accounts for children, either at birth or for an early childhood birthday or other occasion. If that was the case in your family, it's possible that you might not even know about it. How would you know, unless you'd been told? It's possible that the person who opened the account doesn't pay much attention to it because it's not a great deal of money. Or, he or she might have wanted to hold the account for you until you were older and could take control of it.

I'd bet that you don't have half a million dollars sitting around in some account waiting for you, but I wouldn't be too surprised if there was some extra money with your name on it, somewhere. In this chapter, we look at money you might already have, even if you don't know it's there. This will help you to figure out your total assets and your net worth.

Surprise! You Might Have More Than You Know

At this age, you probably don't have a lot of money to call your own unless someone has placed some in trust for you or there are other unusual circumstances that affect you. You might have bank accounts, and of course there's that 57 dollars and 46 cents stashed in your bank on the dresser. But maybe there's some money that you don't know about. Let's consider this enticing possibility, shall we?

Happy Birthday, Honey!

As mentioned a bit earlier in this chapter, friends and rela-tives sometimes open bank accounts for infants and children in the child's name. These accounts normally aren't large (but hey, every little bit counts, right?) and sometimes are over-looked or forgotten, even though they remain open.

Another possibility is that your parents have stashed your birthday money from relatives in a special account earmarked for you. I know that my kids both have bank accounts fund-

ed primarily by $5, $10, $20, and $50 gifts they've
received at birthdays or other holidays. Check it out!

Money Matters

It might seem like too much to hope for, but do ask your
parents if there might be any bank accounts in your name
that you don't know about. A lot of money in banks is left
unaccounted for.

Savings Bonds and So Forth

In addition to bank accounts, you'll need to explore the possibility that there are bonds or stocks in your name. U.S.
savings bonds often are given as birthday presents or contest
prizes. For example, you'll often hear of savings bonds being
given as a prize to the winners of a poetry or writing contest
sponsored by a school or community group. Giving bonds
is a way of giving money that will increase in value over
time. You'll learn more about savings bonds in Chapter 9,
"Making Your Money Work for You."

Some families also give gift shares of stock to children. This is
done to introduce kids to the stock market, get them started
in a financial venture, or sometimes just for fun. Disney
stock is hugely popular among adults buying for kids because
the stock certificates have pictures of Mickey, Minnie, Goofy,
and other Disney friends. Coca-Cola, McDonald's, and Pepsi
are other popular choices among adults who are buying stock
for children.

Make sure you ask whether there might be any stock sitting
around with your name on it. Be especially sure to ask about
this if there are members of your family who are very involved in buying and trading stock.

Tracking Down Your Assets

At this point of your life, your assets are probably fairly limited. Assets, by the way, are everything on the positive side of your balance sheet.

Some common assets are listed here to give you an idea of what they include:

✧ **Bonds and saving bonds.** Investments you buy with the understanding that you'll get your money back—with interest—at the end of an agreed-upon amount of time. They can be issued by corporations or the government.

✧ **Cash accounts.** Checking and savings accounts are examples.

✧ **Certificates of deposit.** An investment that pays a fixed interest rate if you keep your money there for a specified length of time. (More about these in Chapter 9.)

✧ **Mutual funds.** Investments that pool the money of many investors and place it in stocks, bonds, and other holdings. (More about these in Chapter 16, "The Wonderful World of Investments.")

✧ **Stocks.** Investments that represent a piece of ownership in a company. (More about stocks in Chapter 16.)

✧ **Limited partnerships.** A type of legal agreement that allows someone to invest in a business without having to be involved in the day-to-day operations.

✧ **Tax refunds.** A government reimbursement to people who've paid more taxes than they owe.

✧ **Treasury bills.** A bond or note you buy from the U.S. Treasury that pays you interest.

✧ **Cash-value life insurance.** A type of life insurance in which part of the premium is used to provide death benefits and part of it is available to earn interest.

Look over the preceding list and see if any of these categories apply to you. Chances are you'll find at least one or two. Keep them in mind as we move on to consider net worth.

Money and investments earmarked for retirement also must be included when figuring assets:

✧ **Annuities.** Sources of income that come as equal payments at predetermined intervals. They're most often associated with insurance companies and retirement programs.

✧ **Individual Retirement Account (IRA).** (More about these in Chapter 16.)

✧ **Keogh account.** Another type of retirement savings program.

✧ **Pension.** Money received from an employer-sponsored retirement plan.

You can see that most of these don't apply to you. Most teenagers don't own a home, receive annuities, or participate in a limited-partnership agreement. Still, it's interesting to know what's involved when considering what you might have on the plus side.

Figuring Out Your Net Worth

Your *net worth*—strictly speaking in financial terms—is what you get when you add up all your financial assets, such as those listed previously, and subtract all your financial liabilities.

To understand what that means, you need to know about financial liabilities. Hopefully, your liabilities include nothing more serious than the $10 you borrowed from your brother last week. Some teens, though, have already managed to incur more serious liabilities, which negatively affect their net worth.

Money Matters

If you earned enough money during the year that you have to pay federal income tax, the money you have to pay is listed as a liability against your net worth.

Total assets – total liabilities = net worth.

Some common financial liabilities (most of which don't apply to teenagers but might be interesting for you to see) are listed in the following:

- ✧ **Alimony.** Payment one spouse makes to another in the event of a divorce.
- ✧ **Child support.** Payment made by either parent to support a child or children who are living with the other parent or another guardian.
- ✧ **Personal loans.** Money owed to an individual such as the $10 you owe to your brother.
- ✧ **Bank loan.** Money borrowed from a bank.
- ✧ **Car loans.** Money borrowed from a car dealership, bank, or other lending source with the specific intent of purchasing a vehicle.
- ✧ **College loans.** Money borrowed for education.
- ✧ **Credit card bills.** Money owed to pay for purchases made with a credit card. You'll learn much more about these nasty things in Chapter 15, "Understanding Credit Cards and Debt."
- ✧ **Furniture loans.** Loan from the store where you bought the furniture or another lender affiliated with that store.

✧ **Life insurance loans.** Money borrowed against the value of a life insurance policy.

✧ **Pension plan loans.** Money borrowed against the value of a pension plan.

Scary Stuff

Credit card debt is a liability that affects millions of people. Carrying a lot of credit card debt can drastically reduce your net worth, so think about that the next time you're tempted to buy something with your Visa card.

Liabilities involved with real estate also must be included:

✧ **Residence.** This would be a mortgage, including a second mortgage or a line of credit.

✧ **Income property.** Again, if you owe on a mortgage for the property.

✧ **Vacation home.** If you have a mortgage on it, it's considered a liability.

Taxes owed must be included as financial liabilities:

✧ **Capital gains tax.** Tax on profits from the sale of an investment or asset such as stock or real estate.

✧ **Income tax.** Tax on the money you earn during the year.

✧ **Property tax.** Tax assessed on real estate, usually by a municipality or school district.

As you get older, you'll normally acquire more liabilities such as a car payment, college loans, and maybe a mortgage. Your taxes will be higher, and taxes count as liabilities. The good thing, however, is that you'll presumably be earning enough money to offset the liabilities.

To be in good financial health, your assets must total more than your liabilities. Or, for you to be okay financially, your assets absolutely can't be more than your liabilities. With good money management and a bit of luck, your liabilities will be few and your assets many.

Is There Money in Your Future?

We've already discussed the possibility of assets existing in your name such as bank accounts, bonds, or stocks. If someone has, indeed, set up an account or purchased bonds or stock on your behalf, they might have intended for you to get the money at a specified time.

Many parents, grandparents, friends, and other relatives establish trust funds, which provide money or other assets to the child when he or she reaches a certain age. The person who establishes the trust fund probably will designate the age at which the assets should be dispersed.

A *trust* is a legal document, similar to a will, that holds money, property, or other assets for the beneficiary to receive at a designated time in the future. Trust funds can be set up at banks, credit unions, or savings and loans. Some mutual funds also offer trust funds. The institution holding the trust fund determines how much money is required to start the fund, the amount of interest it will pay on money in the fund, and restrictions of withdrawals.

Another way, although a sad one, that you might receive money in the future is if you're included in someone's will. A will is a legal document that instructs how a person's assets are to be divided at the time of his or her death. It also might contain special instructions about how the assets are to be treated or information concerning disposal of the person's body, funeral services, and so forth.

Money Matters

Money kept in trust for a child can be dispersed in one lump sum, or can be given at intervals specified by the person who established the fund.

You also might someday receive money in the form of scholarships or grants intended for your education. This type of money almost always comes with stipulations and instructions, so don't get any ideas about using your scholarship money to run off to Europe and spend the summer picking grapes in a French vineyard.

Knowing that you have some money safely tucked away or that there's money designated for you sometime in the future can provide a great sense of security. It allows you a bit more freedom with the money you earn now, either from allowance or a job you might have.

Don't, however, get lazy and depend on money that might have been placed somewhere in your name, and don't ever depend on money that you might—but might not—receive in the future. Many people have counted on inheritances that, for one reason or another, never materialized.

To figure out just how much money you have, count what you earn and any other possible sources. Consider carefully to determine if there's any money you might not know about, such as money that's been placed in trust for you, or that's in an account you don't know about. Even if there's money in your name that's not available to you now, it's nice to know that it's waiting for you.

The Least You Need to Know

✧ You might have assets that, for one reason or another, you know nothing about.

✧ These unknown assets could be in the form of bank accounts or investments such as stocks or bonds.

✧ Assets are everything that affect your net worth in a positive way; liabilities are everything that affect it in a negative way.

✧ Your total assets, minus your total liabilities, equal your net worth.

✧ Consider the possibility of future sources of money but don't depend on them.

Part 3
Smart Saving

You've probably heard throughout your whole life that it's important to save money. If not, you'll hear it here. The more money you can save when you're young, the better off you'll be later in life; and the more options you'll have when it comes to buying a car, or a house, or helping to pay for educational expenses.

What you're able to save, obviously, is based on how much money you earn and what your expenses are. For that reason, there's no magic formula for saving. Everyone has different circumstances.

Regardless of the amount you're able to stash away, you need to know the best vehicles for saving, and how to make the most of whatever money you have. In this part, we look at different kinds of savings accounts, and even better ways to save and make your money work for you.

Chapter 7

Saving Money Isn't Always Easy

In This Chapter

✧ Understanding financial personality

✧ The difference between savers and spenders

✧ Determining your financial personality

✧ Learning to make saving easier

✧ Convincing reasons to start saving now

Saving money is a good idea. In fact, it's a great idea to save and invest money when you're young so that you'll have it when you really need it. Some people manage to save money easily. It seems to come naturally to them. Others struggle to put even a little bit aside. Their natural tendency is to spend, spend, spend and worry about the consequences later.

In this chapter, we look at how people differ when it comes to saving and spending money. Why is it so much easier for you to stash away $5 or $10 a week in savings than it is for your brother? Or, why does every penny that comes your way seem to fly right back out of your hands the minute you walk into a store? Just as there are different types of personalities, there are different types of financial personalities as well.

Why Some People Find It Harder to Save

There are different theories about how a person's temperament and personality relate to the way he or she handles money, but one thing is for sure: People are as different about money as they are about most other things in life. Some people are impulsive and act spontaneously. Some are more reserved and controlled. Some people believe in living for the moment; others carefully plan out their lives. Some people are constantly afraid, whereas others are undaunted by life's challenges and ups and downs. These different personality traits definitely can affect the way a person handles his or her finances.

Let's consider Bobby for a minute. Bobby is a great person—outgoing, fun to be around, and extremely social. One of Bobby's favorite things to do is hang out at the mall with his friends, and he does so often. They walk up and down the mall, checking out new stores and stopping at their old favorites to make sure they haven't changed.

Scary Stuff

We're sometimes tempted to look down on a person with poor financial habits, but we shouldn't. It could be that he or she has just never learned the importance of smart money handling.

The problem is that Bobby finds it very difficult to control his spending when he's out with his friends. When he sees something at the mall that he likes, he buys it—every time. He doesn't plan to spend; in fact, he tells himself every time that he goes to the mall that he won't buy anything that day.

Somehow, though, he always comes home with a PlayStation game, a new baseball cap, or whatever.

Katie, on the other hand, goes to the mall only when there's a specific item—let's say a particular CD—that she wants to buy. She'll check out three stores to see which has the best price on the CD, buy it, and leave the mall. She's completely in control of her spending. Katie's trip to the mall is an errand, not a social occasion. She knows how much money she has to spend and what she wants to buy. All that's left to do is find the best price and complete the transaction.

People who know what it's like to not have much money sometimes develop peculiar financial personalities.

People affected by hard times such as those of the Great Depression sometimes become hoarders and savers, determined to never be without money again. Other people who survive financial hardship turn in the opposite direction and become great spenders to compensate for the lean times.

In short, nobody knows for sure where and how different people develop their attitudes toward money. We do know that people view money and finances very differently and that the way they handle their money can be either a good or bad thing. You probably can figure out your financial personality pretty easily by looking at the way you handle your money. Knowing why you have that particular personality, however, is much more difficult.

Think back to how you handled birthday gifts of money when you were a little kid. Let's say your Aunt Jennifer has given you $30 on every birthday since you were born. When you were very young, your parents probably handled the money for you. But, as you got older, chances are you began to have some say in what to do with that $30.

If you saved all of it every year, chances are you have a nice little account someplace. Good for you! Maybe you saved half and spent the other half on something you wanted (remember when $15 seemed like a fortune?). Maybe you took the money every year and spent it on Ninja Turtles or clothes for your Barbie dolls.

Imagine That

Just so you know, if you'd saved the $30 every year in a savings account at 4 percent interest, you'd have more than $900 when you turned 20.

The way you handled that money—or other money you might have received or are still getting—will give you some good insights into your financial personality. A quiz in the next section also will help you to determine whether you're a saver or a spender. If you want to know why you have the particular personality you do, you'll need to examine your attitudes and financial background.

What's Your Type?

Let's try to figure out your financial personality by taking a little quiz. Don't worry. This requires no studying, and you don't need to tell anybody else what you get on it.

1. Do you know, within a dollar or two, how much money you have in your possession at this particular moment?

   A. Yes, I know almost to the penny how much I have and where it is.

   B. Haven't got a clue.

2. You've just found a pair of shoes that are to die for, but they cost $60 and aren't on sale:

   A. You decide to wait it out for a week or two and see if they go on sale.

   B. You borrow your mom's credit card and buy them immediately.

3. You get $15 every Sunday to buy your lunches for the following week:

   A. You usually spend only what you have to, and try to save part of the money to use on the weekend.

   B. You're almost always out of money by Wednesday and picking up leftovers from your friends' lunch trays.

4. You go to the drugstore down the street to buy a bottle of shampoo and some cream rinse:

   A. You buy the items you went for and leave the store.

   B. You buy not only the shampoo and cream rinse, but end up with body wash, gum, and a magazine.

5. Your next-door neighbor asked you to cut her grass for her and gave you $20. You didn't expect to have this money:

   A. You stash it in your drawer so that it doesn't get mixed up with the money that's in your wallet.

   B. You call your girlfriend and ask her if you can take her out to dinner that night.

6. You and your friends love movies, but you don't like the admission prices:

   A. You opt to wait to see some of the movies until they get to second-run theaters, or even until they come out on video.

   B. You go to the movies you want to see as soon as they come out so that you can tell everyone about them.

7. You're looking for a dress for the holiday dance at your boyfriend's school, but the only ones that you like cost more than $125 and you don't even know anyone at this school except your boyfriend:

    A. You decide to wear the same dress you wore for your school's holiday dance, even though your boyfriend will see it twice.

    B. You decide that you simply must have a new dress, so you buy one of the expensive ones even though you know you'll only wear it once.

8. Your friends ask you to go with them to dinner at the new café that just opened in your neighborhood. You know that if you go, you won't have enough money to pay to get into the football game tomorrow night:

    A. You tell your friends you'll have to pass this time, but they should be sure to let you know the next time they go.

    B. You go out to eat, figuring that you'll worry about money for the game tomorrow.

9. You've decided to start saving money to use for a car when you start driving:

    A. You open a special savings account so you can deposit and keep track of all your baby-sitting money to use to buy the car.

    B. You have great intentions to save the money you earn from baby-sitting but somehow by the time you get around to going to the bank, it's gone.

10. You get a clothing allowance and you've decided you really need new sneakers for gym:

    A. You find a moderately priced pair of sneaks, figuring that you'll hang on to some of your clothes allowance for something else. After all, they're only for gym class.

    B. You want to buy some cheap sneaks because they're only for gym class, but somehow the $90 Nikes end up on your feet and you've blown your clothes allowance for another month.

Take a minute and look over your answers to these questions. If you circled mostly A's, your financial personality probably leans toward being responsible with money. You don't find it too difficult to save money, even when you're tempted sometimes to buy something you like.

If you circled mostly B's, however, your financial personality could be a source of potential problems for you. You find it difficult to not spend money, even if you know you should be saving for a specific purpose.

If You're a Saver

Being a saver doesn't make you a better person than someone who loves to spend, but it does mean that you've got a good start toward successfully managing your personal finances. This will become even more important as you get older. Just one thing, though: If you're really inclined toward saving—I'm talking about somebody who never spends a cent—be sure not to get too carried away.

Scary Stuff

If you find saving money difficult, you're by no means alone. About 80 percent of the general population of the United States live paycheck to paycheck with very little, if any, savings.

Saving money is good. Never having any fun because you don't want to spend any money is not. Remember that there are no guarantees in life. Not all of us will live to be 100, or 80, or 60, or even 40. It's important to enjoy every day that we have, and although starting to save money while you're young is a great idea and a good way to ensure financial security in the future, having no fun while you're young is a really bad idea. Just be sure that your saving habits aren't out of balance with being a teenager and having a good time.

If You're a Spender

If you're a spender, don't get upset. You're still young, and there's a lot to be said for enjoying yourself and living for the moment. The only problem is that living too much for the moment now means you'll have less to live with later on. One piece of advice that nearly all financial advisors agree on is that the earlier you start saving, the better off you'll be.

You have the great advantage of time when it comes to saving, and even little bits saved now will add up for the future.

Money Matters

If you have trouble keeping track of where you spent your money, try carrying a small notebook with you for a week and recording every penny you spend. Note every pack of gum, every soda—everything. This will give you a clear picture of how much you're spending—and on what.

Ways to Make Saving Money Easier

Being aware of your spending patterns and habits and evaluating purchases before you lay down your money will help you to think more about spending and saving. If you really think about it, you might discover that you spend a lot of money on things you not only don't need, but don't even really want. The next time you're tempted to buy another bottle of nail polish, ask yourself if you really need it or even want it. Chances are the answers to both questions will be "no." I mean, 30 different bottles of nail polish might not only be unnecessary, but a real pain to deal with. You've got to find a place to keep them and move them around to get to other things, and you usually only wear one color at a time, right?

Big Reasons to Start Saving Now

How old are you? Fifteen? Sixteen? Seventeen? Whatever the number, you're young. I know. You feel sometimes as if you've been around forever; but really, you're just getting started. Although your age makes you lucky in many ways, you're especially lucky in terms of your ability to save money. You've got years ahead of you to make your money grow and work for you.

Obviously, the earlier you start saving money, the better off you'll be when you're older. It's hard to think about being 65 or 70 when you're still a teenager, but believe me, it's true that time flies. When you're 65 or 70 and able to travel, lie on a beach, play golf, or shop, you'll be really glad that you started saving money early. In fact, if you start saving money early and continue to do so, you might not have to wait until you're 65 or 70 to start enjoying it.

Consider this: Jessica gets out of college and lands a good job with a big advertising agency. She's really excited because it's exactly the kind of job she'd hoped for, and she's earning $40,000 a year to start. Not bad, right? Jessica is smart about her money, so she starts investing $2,000 each year in a diversified portfolio that earns her a 10 percent compound rate of return (you'll learn more about investing in Chapter 16— all that fancy language means is that Jessica's getting 10 percent interest on her money).

If she throws in $2,000 every year from the time she's 21 until she's 29, and then doesn't put in any more money, she'll have $839,396 in that account when she turns 65. That's $839,396 from an original investment of $18,000.

By starting to save or invest when you're young, you not only set yourself up for financial comfort when you're older, you give yourself a lot more options along the way. Because you have money already saved, you have the luxury of having more money to use for other things—such as a new home or sending kids to college.

The Least You Need to Know

✧ Saving money is smart, but it's a lot harder for some people to do than for others.

✧ Many factors contribute to a person's financial personality.

✧ Most people are either savers or spenders.

✧ Keeping track of your money and being more aware of your spending habits can help make saving easier.

✧ The earlier you start to save, the better off you'll be.

Chapter 8

How Much Should You Save?

In This Chapter

✧ Determining how much you can save

✧ Factors that affect how much you'll save

✧ Looking at what's left after expenses

✧ Sticking to your savings plan

✧ Making sure you pay yourself first

How much money should you save? Two dollars a week? Ten dollars? Fifteen? People struggle endlessly to figure out how much they should be saving. They work hard to strike the perfect balance between how much they spend and how much they put away for the future. They feel guilty for dipping into their savings to buy something they really want. Or, they don't feel guilty and keep dipping into their savings anyway.

Trying to figure out how much money to save can be confusing, but there's really no reason to get stressed about how much to stash away. How much you save is a personal decision based on your own situation and the factors that affect it. In this chapter, we discuss how much money you should save and take a closer look at the benefits of starting to save now, while you're very young and your savings have time to add up into big bucks down the road.

Looking For a Magic Formula

If you're looking for a magic formula for savings, you won't find it here. That's because, at your age, there isn't one. Some teens probably have the means to save $100 a week, whereas others can save nothing because they don't earn anything, or expenses make it impossible for them to save.

Imagine That

The average American saves about 4 percent of his or her annual income. That's less than what some money planners recommend, but definitely better than nothing.

Some money planners say you should save at least 5 to 10 percent of your take-home pay, and that certainly would be desirable. In fact, it's desirable to save as much of your pay as you can. How much you'll save, however, depends on various factors, such as how much you earn, the expenses you have, and how motivated you are to save.

Let's have a look at these factors to see how they affect your ability to save and the amount you'll be able to save.

How Much You Earn

It's pretty much a no-brainer to figure out that what you're able to save depends a lot on how much money you earn. A lot of teenagers, for whatever reasons, don't have outside sources of income. That is, they don't have jobs that pay.

Others, however, love to earn money and might even have more than one part-time job.

Money Matters

Remember that allowance counts as income. Even if it's your only source of money, you can still save some of it if you're committed to doing it.

Teens who work and earn money have greater ability to save than those who don't; unless, of course, you have another source of money such as regular payments from your fabulously wealthy great-aunt who's taken a special interest in your financial future. No wealthy great-aunt in your family, either? Oh, well. Notice I said that working teens have a greater ability to save than nonworkers. However, that doesn't necessarily mean that all working teens save money.

Money Matters

The only money you can save is that which you don't spend, either on things you must pay for or on things you choose to buy.

Expenses

You learned in the last chapter that some people find it easier to save money than others, and teenagers are no exceptions. Some of you, no doubt, have a lot more trouble earmarking money for your savings account than others. You'd much rather take your whole paycheck over to the mall and see what's new at Old Navy or American Eagle.

Some people find it difficult to save money because they like to spend it. Others find it difficult to save money because they have to spend it. You can earn $100 a week, but if you're responsible for paying room and board to your parents and buying all your clothes and everything else you need, you're not going to have much money left to take to the bank and stick into your savings account.

On the other hand, you can make $25 a week, and be able to save $24.50 if your only expense every week is a pack of gum from the drug store. It's great to save money, there's no question about it. The only money you're able to save, however, is that which you don't spend.

If you choose to spend all your money and don't save a cent, shame on you. However, if you can't save money because you must spend all that you make, there's little you can do about it. Wait until you get a pay increase, or try to cut your expenses. Whatever you do, don't increase your expenses unless your pay increases as well.

Incentives for Saving

If your parents told you when you were 12 that they'd match whatever money you managed to save for a car by the time you turned 16 or 17, I'd say you have pretty strong incentive to save all the money you can. Maybe you and your friends have been planning since you were in tenth grade to rent a place at the beach for a week as soon as you graduate. Ten of you will be staying in a house that costs $1,500 to rent, so you'll need $150 plus spending money. That, too, is a strong incentive for saving.

Incentive to save money isn't much different from incentive to do anything else. We can force ourselves to do pretty much anything, but it's a lot more fun—and a lot easier—to do something for which you can see a good reason.

If you're having trouble saving money, think about whether you have some incentive to do so. Saving your money for something you really want and watching it grow toward your goal can be a lot of fun.

Money Matters

If you're having trouble saving money, try to give yourself an incentive. Think of what it would feel like to walk into the music store and buy that guitar you want with your own money or to buy your parents a really special gift for their 20th wedding anniversary. Provide your own incentive to save.

Future Goals

Saving money to meet future goals is similar to having an incentive to save. You're saving now for something you know you want in the future. It can be a car, your college education, or a brand-new computer of your own. Some teens even start saving money to help pay for their weddings or the homes they hope to buy in 10 years.

Kate Bailey is 21 now, and has replaced the car she bought for herself when she was 16 with money that she saved from babysitting jobs. Bailey, of Malvern, Pennsylvania, says she set a goal of saving enough money to buy a car when she was just 10 years old.

"I used to keep the money I made in a bank in my closet, and when I accumulated $100 or so I would take it to the bank and put it into my savings account," Bailey says. "I never really bought anything with that money because I knew that when I turned 16, I wanted a car." When she turned 16, Bailey bought a used Honda Accord for $5,000. She kept the car for almost five years, then traded it in for another used Honda. You guessed it. Her second car also was funded by money she earned through baby-sitting and other jobs.

Everyone has different goals, some of which are a lot more expensive than others. As you get older, you'll need to start looking at more long-term goals. You might decide you want to retire before you're 60, which requires a lot of savings. You might want to buy a bigger home, or a place at the beach or in the mountains, or get some money put away for your kids' college. As your goals for the future take shape and change, the amount of money you'll need to save and the way you save it also are likely to change.

Scary Stuff

You can talk and talk about the importance of saving money, but if you aren't committed to doing it, you'll find it very difficult. It's just like sticking to an exercise program. It's easy to have good intentions, but finding the commitment to do it often is difficult.

Commitment

A person's commitment to saving money also will affect how much he or she will save. There are several ways that a person can become committed (or not) to saving money. Teens whose families have stressed the importance of saving and managing money usually are more committed toward doing so than those whose families put little value on saving.

If you've watched your folks spend all the money they've ever earned on this or that or the other thing and they've told you all along that college is on you if you choose to attend, you might react in one of a couple of ways. You could follow their example and spend everything you earn, never realizing how important it is to save some money because of their example. On the other hand, you might recognize what they've done and make a commitment to save your money instead of spending it on things you don't need.

Deciding What to Save and Sticking to Your Plan

Once you've considered all the factors that affect your personal ability to save money, you should be able to decide how much is reasonable for you to put away. The way to do that is to add up all your expenses and deduct that amount from the total of your income. Expenses include everything that you spend your money on: clothes, snacks, lunches, dues, entertainment, and so forth.

Once you figure out your true expenses and deduct them from your total income, you'll know how much money you have to work with. Let's say, just as an example, that you earn $46 a week (take-home pay) from your part-time job at the dry cleaning shop. Plus, you help an elderly neighbor do laundry every Saturday morning, for which you get $8. Your total earnings are $54 per week.

Money Matters

Don't assume, if your expenses are high, that they can't be reduced. Cutting expenses is a great way to increase the money you're able to save. You might find that some of the things you consider true expenses will hardly be missed at all if you cut them.

Out of that $54, your expenses might look something like this:

✧ Lunch at school—$2 a day, or $10 a week

✧ A movie and burgers with your friends every Friday night—$12

✧ Offering to your church or synagogue—$3 a week

✧ Miscellaneous—$10 a week

When you total up your expenses ($35) and subtract them from your earnings ($54), you have $19 left. That's the pool of money from which your savings will come.

That doesn't mean that you have to save all of the $19; it just means that $19 is what you have available after deducting your expenses. If you save all of the $19 you have left over, you'd be saving more than one-third of your income. Doing so would put you in great shape down the road, but it might not be feasible to save that big a percentage of your total income. Remember though, as you get older, your expenses will increase along with the amount of money you earn.

It makes good sense to save as much as you can while your expenses are low, even if you're not earning a whole lot of money. As you learned in the last chapter, even a little savings now can add up to big dollars in the future. Even saving $5 or $10 per month adds up if you have it in an account where you're earning interest and the interest is compounded (more about different ways to save and different kinds of interest in Chapter 9, "Making Your Money Work for You").

Consider the following:

✧ If you save just $5 a month in an account that pays 5 percent interest and is compounded quarterly, you'd have $62 at the end of a year; $341 at the end of five years; $779 at the end of 10 years, and $1,340 at the end of 15 years—all that from saving just $5 a week.

✧ If you save $20 a month, or $5 a week, you'd have $250 at the end of one year; $1,365 at the end of five years; $3,115 at the end of 10 years; and $5,359 at the end of 15 years.

✧ If you'd manage to save $100 a month, or $25 a week, you'd have $1,233 at the end of one year; $6,825 at the end of five years; $15,576 at the end of 10 years; and $26,794 at the end of 15 years. Maybe that's enough incentive to get you saving!

Regardless of how much you decide you're able to save, stick with it. Don't decide to take a week or two off from saving because you run into some extra expenses. It's often difficult to give up something you want to do so you can fund your savings account, but it's way worth it in the long run.

Imagine That

Benjamin Franklin is credited with saying, "Money begets money and its offspring begets more." What he was saying is that earning interest on your savings is a good way to keep the savings growing.

Paying Yourself (and Your Savings) First

A good way to think about the money that you designate as savings is to consider it your pay. And you should always, always, always pay yourself first. If you get a paycheck from an employer, you might be able to have money automatically taken out of your pay and placed into your savings account. Check with your bank to see if this is possible. If not, discipline yourself to deposit your savings immediately.

If you think of saving money as doing a favor for yourself, it becomes a lot less of a drag. There's no amount too small to save; even $1 a week will add up. Many people make the mistake of thinking if they can't save $30 or $40 a week, there's no point in saving at all; however, you know differently.

Imagine That

Money that earns 5 percent interest will double itself in a bit more than 14 years. Money that earns 6 percent doubles in 12 years, and money that earns 7 percent doubles in 10 years. It pays to get the best interest rate you can find.

Whatever amount you decide to save will be right for you. Don't try to save more than you're realistically able to do because you'll get frustrated and might not save anything. On the other hand, do save as much as you comfortably can handle. You'll be glad you did.

The Least You Need to Know

✧ Factors that affect how much you'll be able to save include your income, expenses, incentive, goals and commitment.

✧ You need to add up all your expenses and subtract them from your income to find out how much you have left over to use for your savings.

✧ Regardless of what you decide you'll save, it's important to stick with it and save regularly.

✧ Even small amounts of money will add up to significant savings over time.

✧ Thinking of saving money as a payment you make to yourself might make it easier to see your money go into an account, rather than into your wallet.

Chapter 9

Making Your Money Work for You

In This Chapter

✧ Knowing the best ways to save your money

✧ Opening a savings account

✧ Looking at different kinds of financial institutions

✧ The difference between simple and compound interest

✧ Other ways to save your money

Most people agree that having money is a good thing. You've already learned how money not only enables you to get stuff you need or want, but also gives you options and choices and allows you a level of independence that you wouldn't have without it.

What many people might not realize is that having money is just one part of the equation. Knowing how to make the money you have work for you is nearly as important as having it at all. In this chapter, you learn about smart ways to save the money you have and how to get the most back from your money that you can.

Some Ways of Saving Are Better Than Others

How do you save your money? Maybe you have a bank account or you keep your cash in a box on your dresser. Some people just carry all the money they have around with them so that it's readily available when they see something they want to buy. Others give their money to their parents to keep so they won't be tempted to spend it.

There are a lot of ways to save money, but some make a lot more sense than others. If you have $200 and you keep it in a box on your dresser, you'll have $200 until you spend it, somebody in your family borrows it, or your dog eats it. If you have $200 and you put it in an interest-bearing savings account, you'll earn money on your money.

Putting your money someplace where it earns interest is smarter than keeping it in a box on your dresser, under your mattress, or on the top shelf of your closet.

Imagine That

Banks used to pay 5 percent interest on all savings accounts because it was a federal regulation. Unfortunately, along came banking deregulation in 1986, and interest rates have never been the same.

Opening a Savings Account

So, you want to open a savings account? Good! You're definitely on the right track. Before you walk down to the corner bank and hand over all your money, though, let's consider some things you should know about banks and the accounts and services they offer.

Choosing a Bank

Commercial banks have changed tremendously in the past couple of decades. We've seen one bank after another merge with a larger one, change its name, and open under new management, only to merge again a short time later and start the cycle over again. It's a full-time job just keeping up with the names of some of these banks, much less their policies and the people who work in them. It hasn't always been that way with banks.

Money Matters

There are somewhere around 13,000 different commercial banks operating in America today. This is down from about 31,000 during America's banking heyday in the 1920s.

Picture this, if you can: Once upon a time—not all that long ago—people kept their money in small banks in their neighborhoods or towns. They'd go to their banks often, and they were acquainted with the people who worked there. They knew the names of the people who waited on them and the employees knew their names, too. They'd ask about each other's children or discuss the weather. There were no ATM machines in this once-upon-a-time bank land, so customers visited their banks often to make deposits or withdrawals.

It's a lot harder these days to find personal service and customer loyalty in banking, so you might have to look around for a while until you find an institution you like. Mega-mergers, increasingly complicated regulations, and more and more bank fees have discouraged many a person looking for the right bank. (Did you know that some banks actually charge customers to make a face-to-face transaction with a teller?)

You're likely to use the same bank your parents do when opening a savings or other type of account, and that's fine. If your parents are happy with their bank, it's probably a good institution. Just so you know, though, there are some questions you should ask when you're trying to choose a bank:

✧ Must I have a minimum amount with which to open an account?

✧ Will I be charged a monthly fee if I don't maintain a certain balance in my account?

✧ Does the bank charge a fee for me to get my account balances or for other services?

✧ Will I be penalized if I don't keep my money in the account for a certain amount of time?

✧ Is my account federally insured?

✧ How much interest will I earn on my savings?

✧ How is the interest compounded? (More about that later in the chapter.)

It's smart to compare banks if you're choosing one on your own. You can check out their ads in the newspaper, get information from their Web sites, or even stop by and look them over personally. Don't be discouraged if you have to look at a few different banks before you find one you like. Remember that just because you're young doesn't mean that your savings account isn't important. In fact, a smart bank will go out of its way to attract and keep young investors. After all, you've got loads of potential for earning down the road, and you might someday be one of the bank's most important customers.

Or, Maybe Not a Bank

Commercial banks, although the biggest segment of the U.S. banking system, aren't the only game in town. Generally, there are three types of financial institutions:

✧ Commercial banks

✧ Credit unions

✧ Savings and loans (also called thrifts)

Imagine That

Commercial banks hold nearly three-quarters of all the money in the U.S. banking system. Credit unions and thrifts share the other quarter of total assets.

Commercial banks such as those you read about in the last section are permitted to take deposits, lend money, and provide other banking services. They can have either a federal or a state charter and are regulated depending on which kind they have.

Those with federal charters have to be insured by the Federal Deposit Insurance Corporation (FDIC). This is good for the consumer, because if on the off chance something should happen to your money while it's in the bank, the FDIC will replace it.

Credit unions are alternatives to commercial banks and offer many of the same services. You can set up a savings or checking account, get an ATM card, or take out a certificate of deposit—just like in a regular bank. Because credit unions are nonprofit organizations and don't have to pay federal taxes, they generally can give you better interest rates.

If your parents or other family members belong to a credit union, there's a good chance that you could open a savings account there. You also could check to see if there are any opportunities to join a credit union through your school, church or synagogue, or another group that you belong to.

Thrifts are the third major type of financial institution, commonly called savings and loans (S&Ls). S&Ls were started in the 1930s with the idea of loaning money for people to use to buy homes. They were popular for many years, but fell out of favor with the public in the late 1980s, when many of them had to be bailed out by the federal government.

The good news is that savings and loans have cleaned up their act due to legislative changes, and they're once again considered viable choices for those looking for a place to open an account or conduct other financial business. If you're thinking about putting your money in an S&L, just be sure that it's insured. If you see a sign in the window or on a Web site that says SLIC, your money will be covered.

Imagine That

There are seven Lee Credit Unions in the United States, whose members are many of the approximately 100,000 people in this country who share the last name Lee.

Internet Banks

Internet banks are still new, but experts predict they'll become increasingly important. They work pretty much like traditional banks—you can set up checking and savings accounts, transfer funds, pay bills, and make withdrawals—only it's almost all done online. Instead of writing out a slip to transfer funds from one account to another and handing it to the bank teller, you click your mouse to go to the appropriate places.

To deposit money into an online account, you usually can send a check and a deposit slip to the bank's physical address. Or, you can wire deposit money from another bank or have your paycheck directly deposited into your account. Most Internet banks will give you an Automatic Teller Machine (ATM) card to use to get money from your account, or you can write a check for withdrawals.

Money Matters

To learn more about Internet banks and banking online, check out the Motley Fool Web site at www.fool.com/money/banking/online.

You also can get a credit card from an Internet bank. The appeal of Internet banks for many people is the convenience of being able to conduct your banking business whenever you want to, without having to leave your home. We'll be hearing and seeing a lot more about Internet banking in the near future.

Finding the Best Kind of Account

Once you've decided where you want to put your money, you'll have to decide what kind of account to open. If you're going to be using your money and will need access to it, you'd probably be better off opening a checking account than a savings account. If that's the case, look around a bit and see if you can find a bank that pays interest on checking accounts. They're pretty rare these days, but there are a few around. You'll learn a lot more about when and how to open a checking account in Chapter 13, "The Great Balancing Act."

If you're putting your money in the bank with the intention of letting it sit there for a while, a savings account is what you need. Be sure you check out what interest rates various banks are offering and any regulations that apply to the account, and be sure to find out how the bank compounds its interest.

The Miracle of Compound Interest

There's no question about it: Saving money can be a drag, especially when you're first starting out. Interest doesn't accumulate very fast on small amounts of savings, and watching your savings grow can be almost as frustrating as being grounded over a holiday weekend. Eventually, however, the interest you get on your savings will cause them to grow. Of course, the more money you have in an account, the more interest you'll get—and the kind of interest you get counts, too.

Simple Interest

Simple interest pays you the stated rate on the money you have in your savings account—period. If you have $2,000 in your account, for instance, and the interest rate is 3 percent, you'll earn $60 on your money at the end of the year. If you have $10,000 in your account, you get $300.

Interest is great, because it lets your money work for you. The more money you save, the more interest you earn. Simple interest, which we usually just call interest, is good. However, compound interest is even better.

Compound Interest

Compound interest is better than simple interest because it lets you earn not only on the money you've saved, but on the interest you get on that money—it gives you interest on your interest. Interest usually is compounded (or added up) in one of several ways. It can be continuous: daily, weekly, monthly, quarterly, or yearly. The more often interest is compounded, the more you get. If you're getting 3 percent interest on $1,000 every month and then earning interest on your interest, you'll be further ahead at the end of the year than if the interest is compounded only quarterly or annually.

So, when you're looking for a bank to take your hard-earned baby-sitting or paper route money, look for one that compounds interest most frequently. It really can make a difference as your money grows.

Imagine That

If you invested $10 a week in an account that paid 8 percent compound interest (we'll tell you where to find these accounts in the next section) from the time you were 10 until you were 30, you'd have $43,041. About three-quarters of that amount is interest.

Looking Beyond Savings Accounts

After you've accumulated money in a savings account for a while and you have a substantial amount, it's a good idea to think about moving those savings to another type of account. There's no point in earning just 2 percent on your money if you can earn 7 or 8 percent. Even if you have just $100, you'd be earning $7 or $8 a year as opposed to $2. If you have $1,000, the difference would be $70 or $80 a year as opposed to $20. You don't need a degree in economics to figure out which is the better deal. Let's look at a few other ways to save money that generally pay more interest than a regular savings account.

Money Market Accounts

Money market accounts are considered to be a type of savings account, but they generally pay a bit more interest than the regular ones. They're interesting because you can write checks on the account, sort of like with a checking account. If you need to have checks available but write only a couple each month, it might make sense for you to have a money market account. If you don't use checks at all, or you need to write more than two or three per month, a different kind of account might be better. You're usually allowed to write three checks per month on a money market account; any more than that and you have to pay a fee.

105

Imagine That

For some reason, there were some banks in Atlanta that paid up to 25 percent interest on money market accounts in the early 1980s. Wouldn't you have loved to have had your money in one of those accounts?

When money market accounts were created in the early 1980s, you could earn 10 percent or more interest on the money you invested in them. Of course, they were extremely popular, but the high interest didn't last. The interest rates paid on money market accounts have fluctuated in the past 20 years, but never got back up to where they started. Some banks require a minimum amount for opening a money market account, while others require that a minimum balance (often around $2,000) be kept in the account in order to earn interest on your money. It varies from bank to bank, so be sure to check if you're interested in opening this sort of account.

Certificates of Deposit

If you hear somebody in a bank talking about CDs, chances are they mean certificates of deposit, not compact discs. CDs are a good way to earn more interest than you do with a regular account, but you need to have a minimum amount to open one, and you get penalized if you need to get your money out before the CD comes due.

Here's how a CD works: You deposit your money for a specified amount of time, usually between three months and several years. Some kinds of CDs require $1,000 or more to get started, but there are others that require $500 or even less. If your savings account has become substantial and you don't think you'll be needing the money in it anytime soon, you should look into opening a CD.

Check out the financial pages of your Sunday paper to get the CD interest rates in your area. That information also should include the minimum balance you need to open one.

Imagine That

If you do open a CD at your bank, be sure to ask whether there are any incentives associated with it. Some banks waive bank machine or checking account fees if you open a CD with them. It doesn't hurt to ask!

Savings Bonds

There are different kinds of bonds, but what you might already have, or might want to consider purchasing, are U.S. savings bonds. Savings bonds are great gifts, and as mentioned in Chapter 6, "Money You Might Already Have," you might have savings bonds that somebody purchased for you and stashed away.

Bonds are an investment, but they're a lending investment, as opposed to an ownership investment such as stocks. When you buy a bond, you're lending your money to an organization such as the U.S. government or a corporation. The organization uses your money and, in exchange, promises that it will give you your money back—along with some interest on it—after an agreed-upon amount of time.

Some types of bonds are issued by the federal government, and some by corporations. Municipal bonds are issued by state, local, or county governments, or by a nonprofit organization such as a hospital or college.

107

U.S. savings bonds are a safe investment because they come from the government and are guaranteed by the government. This is how they work: You buy a $100 Series E savings bond (that's the most common kind of U.S. bond) from your bank or other financial institution. The neat thing is you pay only $50 for it. You earn interest on your savings bond and, if you hold it for a certain amount of time, you'll get $100 when you turn it in.

If you have money to save, by all means, save it. It's hard to think about it when you're a teenager, but someday you'll be middle-aged and thinking about retirement, or even (gasp!) elderly and long since retired. By starting to save money now, you can ensure a more comfortable and secure life for yourself later.

The Least You Need to Know

❖ Saving money any way you can is good, but using a method of saving that pays you interest is better than one that doesn't.

❖ Opening a savings account is a common and beneficial way to save money because it's easy to do and it pays interest.

❖ Banks are the most common kind of financial institution, but there are also credit unions and savings and loans.

❖ Compound interest is preferable to simple because it pays you interest on your interest.

❖ Money market accounts, certificates of deposit, and savings bonds are other ways to save money and let it work for you.

Part 4

Smart Spending

Let's face it: For most of us, spending is the fun part about having money. Spending too much, however, cuts into what we can save, and can jeopardize our financial health. A budget can help you take control of your spending and keep your finances organized and on track. Budgets are a good idea for everyone, even though most people don't like the thought of using one.

Whether or not you're operating within a budget, be aware that some methods of spending money make a lot more financial sense than others. Why buy something when it's in season if you can wait until the season passes and get it for half price? Why pay full price for an item that will be on sale in the department store that very weekend?

This part fills you in on smart strategies for spending, or not spending, your money. We also take a look at a big expense you might be anticipating or already dealing with—a car.

Chapter 10

Budgets Are for Everybody

In This Chapter

✧ The wildly unpopular budget

✧ Understanding why budgets are good

✧ Including necessities and non-necessities

✧ Anticipating nonroutine expenses

✧ Cutting back when you need to

Planning a budget and sticking to it might seem like a big-time drag, but chances are you'll be happier and better off money-wise in the long run if you do it. Hardly anybody looks forward to having to plan and sticking to a budget. I mean, really, who wouldn't rather have plenty of money to go out and get whatever you want instead of worrying about how much you're spending? The truth is, though, that most of us do have to plan our spending. Chances are pretty good that by now you've learned there's never enough money to get everything you'd like to have.

It's hard enough to have some change left over at the end of the week during regular spending times, but then along come those out-of-the-ordinary circumstances that really stress the old pocketbook. Your girlfriend's and your mom's birthdays that happen to be only four days apart, holiday presents for your family, the junior prom for which you simply must have a new dress and shoes—you know what I'm saying. These and other must-buy situations can really stretch, or even deplete, your financial reserves.

However, following a budget can go a long way toward ensuring that you'll have money when you need it. That doesn't mean you'll have unlimited supplies of the green stuff. It means that if you know what you have, know what you need, and plan what you'll spend, you'll be financially cool.

Why Nobody Likes a Budget

Budgets are kind of like going to the dentist. You probably don't like to do it, but you know that you should because it's good for you. Budgets have a bad rep, mostly because they require a degree of discipline. If you stick to one, it sometimes might force you to say "I guess not" to things you'd really like to have.

It's tough to put off getting something that you really want. We live in a society where instant gratification is the way to go. Get it now and pay later. Charge it. Don't worry about it until the bill comes. If you've fallen into the gotta-have-it-now rut, living within a budget won't be easy. If you can do it, though, you'll be on the fast track to financial success.

The Benefits of Budgeting

Learning to use a budget while you're young has some important advantages. The most immediate is that you'll learn to handle the money you have now. A more long-range advantage, but probably even more important, is that you'll establish good spending and saving habits for down the road.

Let's face it: If you get into financial trouble now, there's a good chance that somebody will be able to bail you out.

Mom or Dad will cover you or your best bud will loan you a few bucks to see you through until allowance time.

However, 10 or 15 years from now, chances are you'll be out in the real world and living on your own. You're likely to have a job, an income, a car, an apartment or house, maybe even a spouse and a family. You'll also have annoying little money issues such as taxes, utility bills, credit card bills, insurance bills, more bills, and more bills.

Scary Stuff

By age 25, the average American is $6,000 in debt—not a good financial position! Learning to budget and control your finances now can give you a huge advantage as you get older.

Learning to take care of your money now will go a long way toward ensuring that you'll do it later in life—when it really counts. Let's make it plain; setting up and using a budget is a good idea for the following reasons:

✧ Having a budget puts you in control of your finances and helps you avoid money pitfalls. It forces you to look at what you spend your money on and will tell you exactly what you can spend each week or month at the mall, at Burger King, or whatever.

✧ Having a budget now teaches you good financial habits that you'll be able to use for the rest of your life.

Now, let's get down to business and see what a budget for a person your age might look like.

What to Include in Your Budget

If you're one of the growing number of teenage entrepreneurs who have already started and are running a successful small business (more about these creatures in Chapter 17, "Thinking About a Business of Your Own"), or you get a huge allowance each week, or you have different means of income and varied expenses, you might want to consider getting some electronic help in tracking your cash. There are a bunch of computer software programs designed to make keeping track of income and expenses easier. Some of the most popular ones are Quicken, Microsoft Money, and Managing Your Money.

Money Matters

There's really no right way or wrong way to set up a budget. It's more a matter of figuring out what works for you. It can be simple or complicated, but you've got to be comfortable with it and able and willing to use it.

However, if you're a typical teen, you probably don't need electronic help to set up a budget. In fact, your budget probably will be pretty simple, because your income and expenses probably are pretty limited.

The first thing you need to do is to get a handle on what you're making and on how you're spending your money. We discussed where your money comes from in Part 2, "So, How Are You Gonna Get It?" so think back to what you read and come up with a total of any and all income you have. This includes money you might get for allowance, doing yard work for a neighbor, baby-sitting, gifts from grandparents, and so forth.

The next step is to figure out how you spend your money—
and this probably will be a little harder. Most of us spend significant amounts of money on small items, many of which
we don't even remember once the money is gone. Take a few
minutes to think about spending categories—that is, general
categories within which you spend. Some examples of spending categories include:

✧ Housing (probably doesn't apply)

✧ Transportation (your own wheels, bus fares, gas for
Dad's car, and so forth)

✧ Debt (may or may not apply, depending on whether
you have a credit card, student loans, or whatever)

✧ Entertainment

✧ Personal expenses

✧ Charities

You'll need to list and expand on these expense categories,
and try to figure out how much you spend on each. Most
people work with monthly budgets, but if it works better for
you to operate week by week, that's fine, too. Don't worry if
you don't know exactly how much you spend, just get as
close as you can. This will help you to see what you're spending and to look at ways you can cut back in certain areas or
shift spending to other areas.

The following is an example of a budget with limited expenses that a typical teenager might use. Feel free to adapt this
sample to fit your own needs. Just take out any categories
that don't apply to you.

A Sample Budget Worksheet for Teens

Item	Approximate Amount Spent
Housing	
Rent	$
Utilities	$

continues

A Sample Budget Worksheet for Teens (continued)

Item	Approximate Amount Spent
Housing	
Phone	$
Cable	$
Furniture	$
Appliances	$
Maintenance	$
Total:	$
Transportation	
Gas	$
Car maintenance	$
License/taxes	$
Public transportation	$
Insurance	$
Total:	$
Debt	
Credit card	$
Car loans	$
Student loans	$
Personal loans	$
Line of credit	$
Total:	$
Entertainment	
Movies, concerts, etc.	$
Vacation	$
Hobbies	$
Pets	$
Magazines, books	$

Item	Approximate Amount Spent
Entertainment	
Videos, CDs, cassettes, etc.	$
Restaurants, fast food	$
Total:	$
Personal	
Clothes	$
Shoes	$
Jewelry	$
Cosmetics, personal care items	$
Gifts	$
Other	$
Total:	$
Charity	$
Church/synagogue	$
Other	$
Total:	$
Grand Total:	$

Necessities First

When you're making a budget, the first expenditures you need to include are the ones that are necessary. If you have things that you're definitely and ultimately responsible for paying, don't even think about eliminating that money within your budget.

Right now, however, you probably don't have many necessary expenses. Your Friday night foray to the Outback Steakhouse doesn't count as necessary, even though it might seem that way to you.

If you're responsible for buying your own clothing, shoes, or toothpaste, those are necessary expenses. If you're responsible for paying for costs associated with school, such as any out-of-the-ordinary fees for supplies, that's a necessary expense. If you have a car and are responsible for its upkeep and insurance, those are necessary expenses. If you're living in an apartment, housing costs certainly are a necessary expense. The more independently you're living, the more necessary expenses you'll have. Be sure you budget for them before you budget for anything else.

As you get older and your financial responsibilities increase, you'll have a lot more of these necessary expenses. They include things such as housing, debt, insurance, taxes, transportation, health care, and costs of raising kids.

Nonessentials Second

Once you've budgeted for all the necessities (be sure you don't forget anything), you can start thinking about the nonessentials. These expenses include stops at the donut shop on your way to school, the baseball cap with the logo of your favorite team, dinners with your friends—all the things you like to have and to do, but don't really need.

If most of your needs are taken care of by your parents or whomever, any money you have can be used toward things that you want.

Understanding Budget Terms

There are various terms used to describe different aspects of a budget. Not all of these terms will apply to a budget for someone your age, but it doesn't hurt for you to know what the following mean:

✧ **Routine expenses.** These are the expenses that remain relatively the same, week after week, or month after month. They might include rent, insurance, food, and entertainment.

✧ **Nonroutine expenses.** Nonroutine expenses are easy to forget about, because they don't occur regularly. They might include medical bills, car repairs, wedding gifts, and so forth.

✧ **Fixed expenses.** These are costs that don't vary much in amount from month to month (or whatever time period you're using). They include rent, car payments, health club dues, and so forth.

✧ **Variable expenses.** Expenses that are variable change from month to month. They might include entertainment costs, vacations, food, clothing, and utilities.

✧ **Nondiscretionary expenses.** These are the necessary ones—the ones you can't get away from. They include housing, food, utilities, taxes, car payments, and so forth.

✧ **Discretionary expenses.** If an expense is discretionary, it's not necessary. They include vacations, memberships, entertainment, and so forth.

There are combinations of these types of expenses. For instance, a discretionary expense can be either fixed or variable. A health club fee is a fixed, discretionary expense. It's the same each month, but it's not necessary. Rent is a fixed, nondiscretionary, routine expense. A vacation is a variable, discretionary, nonroutine expense. You get the idea, right?

Factoring In Nonroutine Expenses

If you're setting up a budget for yourself, you'll need to think ahead to anticipate the nonroutine expenses that might come up. This can be a lot of fun, because it allows you to imagine all kinds of neat possibilities.

Maybe your girlfriend's family will invite you to go along on their vacation to the beach like they did last year. You know it's not a given, but it could happen. If it does, you'll probably want to have some extra cash put aside to take along. Or,

119

maybe some senior is selling the snowboard of your dreams, for half of what you'd have to pay for it new. If you've anticipated for nonroutine expenses within your budgets, you can be heading for the slopes on your new board this weekend.

Money Matters

Nonroutine expenses aren't necessarily big surprises, they're just not routine. For instance, your brother's birthday present is a nonroutine expense, even though his birthday rolls around every year at the same time.

The biggest dance of the year is coming up and you've just seen the greatest dress ever. The problem is that it's super expensive and your mom's not budging from the $65 she promised to put toward it. Having some money allocated for nonroutine expenses in your budget puts you on your way to the mall with enough money to buy the dress.

Of course, whether or not you'll be able to anticipate and save for nonroutine expenses depends on how much income you have, and your other expenses. If you can, though, it's a good idea to try to set some money aside for these types of things.

Trimming the Fat from Your Budget

Once you've listed all your expenses, compare what you spend to what you earn. Maybe you're in pretty good financial shape—not spending too much, and able to save some money every week or month.

On the other hand, maybe you're surprised to see exactly how much you've been spending. Remember all those little things such as that pack of gum, the double latte, and that great shade of lipstick? Small items sure can add up quickly, can't they? If you're not happy about how your expenditures stack up to your income, you can do one of two things:

✧ Make more money

✧ Spend less money

Money Matters

Almost every budget has spending areas that can be reduced. Look first to entertainment, then to personal items.

If you've already got a job, it might be impractical to think about getting another. Most states have restrictions on how many hours teenagers can work. Besides, you need time to do homework, be with your friends, hang out at home, and pursue other interests and hobbies. You might be able to add on some more hours or find a job that pays more, but remember there's more to your teenage years than making money.

If your earning potential is pretty well maxed out and you're not happy with the amount of money you've been able to put aside, it's time to think about trimming some of the fat from your budget. Trimming the fat can be extremely painful, but trust me, it almost always can be done. You'd be surprised at what you can do without if you really have to.

Although almost any expense included in your budget can be trimmed, some areas are easier to scale down than others. Generally, variable expenses are easier to trim than fixed expenses, and discretionary expenses are easier to cut than nondiscretionary. That's not to say, however, that you can't save money in all areas of your budget. Pay extra attention to categories such as entertainment and personal.

There are a lot of ways to spend less, and a good budget can help you to do so by making you more aware of where your money is going.

Scary Stuff

Don't spend a lot of time drafting a budget, only to have it go by the wayside a month or two later. Many a person has gone off the financial straight and narrow by abandoning budgeting efforts. Stick with it!

The Least You Need to Know

✧ Many people resist setting up and using a budget, but nearly everyone can benefit from one.

✧ Learning to use a budget now will help you get control of your money and establish good financial habits.

✧ Your budget should include various spending areas such as transportation, entertainment, charity, and personal.

✧ It's important to anticipate expenses that don't occur regularly so that you'll be prepared for them.

✧ There are many ways to trim your budget, primarily from areas that include variable and discretionary expenses.

Chapter 11

Getting the Most for Your Money

In This Chapter

✦ Deciding whether or not to buy it today

✦ Buying according to the seasons

✦ Comparing department, discount, and outlet stores

✦ Using alternative methods to buy at great prices

✦ Knowing when to go secondhand

Most teenagers—most everybody, for that matter—have limited amounts of money to spend. That's why we need budgets (remember Chapter 10, "Budgets Are for Everybody"?) to help us spend our money wisely, and discipline to help us hang on to some of that cash we'd like to spend on all the good stuff we see every day.

The issue, then, is how to be smart about spending the money you have. You want to make the most of your money, right? Let's say you have $50. That might sound like a lot until you get into Bloomingdale's and find out there's not a sweater on the rack for less than $48, or that it'll barely be enough for an afternoon on the ski slopes with a burger afterward.

So, how are you going to get your money's worth, no matter how much moola you have? If $20 is all you have, you'd better be darned sure you make the most of it. Ditto for $100, $500, or $1,000. People who are financially savvy make their money work for them, no matter how much of it they have. In this chapter, you learn how to make you money work for you and how to make the most out of what you have.

Deciding What to Buy

Choices, choices, choices. There are so many things to want, and so little money with which to buy. But, that's okay; there are some easy guidelines to follow when shopping that will help you make smart choices when deciding what to buy.

Go For It!

Picture this: You've just seen something in a store that you consider an absolute must-have. You know you're not going to be able to live without it. You check your wallet and, sure enough, you have enough money to buy whatever it is that has you so excited.

Before you rush over and tell the salesperson to get it out of the case and ring it up, take a few minutes to consider what you're doing and whether or not it's really a good idea to buy the watch, the shoes, the CD, or whatever it is that you've fallen for.

Ask yourself the following questions:

1. Do I really need this item that I'm thinking about buying?

2. If I don't need it, do I at least really, really want it?

3. Am I sure that I'll use whatever it is I'm thinking about buying?

4. If I buy it now, will I have enough money for other stuff that I might need or want this week?

5. Will this purchase interfere with my ability to pay off any debts I might have?

6. Will it hurt for me to delay this purchase and buy it later?

7. Is there someplace else where I might be able to buy the same thing for less, or might the item be put on sale soon in this store?

8. Is there an item that's similar to this one, but less expensive, that I might like just as much?

If you think about these questions and answer them honestly, you'll have a good indication of whether or not you should buy the item in question. If you said "yes" to questions 1, 2, 3, 4, and 6, and "no" to questions 5, 7, and 8, chances are this is a good purchase for you.

Money Matters

When you're considering buying something at full price, ask the salesperson if it will be put on sale soon. Many stores have sales every other week or so and you might be able to get it for less if you wait. On the other hand, some brands rarely, if ever, are put on sale.

Your "yes" answers to questions 1 through 3 indicate that you either need or really want the item, and you're sure that you'll use it. A nod to question 4 means that you won't be overspending on this item and have no money left for the rest of the week. And, saying "yes" to question 6 indicates that there's reason to buy the item now instead of waiting. Maybe it's a one-of-a-kind thing and there are no replacements.

Saying "no" to question 5 tells us that you have enough money to take care of paying what you might owe. And answering in the negative to questions 7 and 8 indicate that the item you want isn't available for less someplace else, and won't be going on sale in a few days or weeks. That being the case, go for it!

Not Today, Thanks

Sometimes, after giving some thought to the question of whether or not to buy something, you'll decide to let it go. Maybe you know you don't really need the item, and once you think about it, you realize that you're not all that crazy about it. Maybe you've seen the same thing someplace else for $10 less or you figure it'll be on sale by the end of the month.

Imagine That

Two professors at the University of California at Berkeley analyzed 30,000 purchases of 4,200 consumers in 14 cities and found out that unplanned purchases accounted for 68 percent of items bought while shopping at grocery stores. Let's hear it for impulse buying!

You might be a little concerned about your money situation now and not see the need to make things worse by buying on impulse. If you're unsure about buying something, usually the best thing to do is to let it go. Tell yourself that you'll think about it and come back tomorrow if you still think you want it. You might even ask the salesperson to hold the item for you, just in case you decide you really can't live without it. Chances are if you leave it at the store, you'll come to the realization that you don't need whatever it is you're considering.

Knowing When to Buy

To get the most from your money, you've got to know when to buy as well as what to buy. Some things, such as peaches, tomatoes, and sunscreen, are best bought in season. Other things, such as winter coats, bathing suits, and airline tickets, are best bought out of season.

Buying in Season

In season, you can buy a basket of sweet red peppers at a farm stand for $3. A basketful of the same in January, however, could cost you 10 times that much.

The same idea goes for the sunscreen that was mentioned earlier. If you're going to Florida for spring break, wait until you get there and hit the local discount store. It'll have all kinds of beach stuff, and you won't have to pay a fortune for it. Trying to find sunscreen in the middle of March in New Jersey can be like trying to track down a bikini at the North Pole on Christmas Eve. When it comes to produce and other truly seasonal items, shopping in season is best. Some other things, however, are best purchased out of season.

Money Matters

If you get a craving for raspberries (or whatever) when they're out of season, check out the frozen department. Fruit frozen at the peak of its season usually is pretty good, especially if you're cooking or baking with it.

Buying out of Season

Here's the deal. It's late March, and you swing into your favorite shop to buy a new fleece jacket in a spring color. Your best friend got a hot pink one last week, and your brother's girlfriend just showed up with a great turquoise-colored one.

While you're in the store, you notice that the heavy winter jackets are on sale—big time on sale—like 75 percent off. You can actually buy a warm, but very cool winter jacket for less than you were planning to pay for the spring fleece. And the thing is, you really need a winter coat. The one you wore this season was tight enough to be uncomfortable, not to mention embarrassing because it looks like something your younger sister would wear.

So, what do you do? Buy the winter coat at a steal price and leave the spring jacket? Or buy that pale yellow fleece that will look great with your new jeans on your class spring trip? Take a minute and think about this scenario. Take another minute. Okay. It's time to come out with an honest answer. What would you do?

If you said that you'll buy the winter coat, good for you! Pat yourself on the back and step into the thrifty shopper club, but if you know deep down that you'd buy the fleece and worry about a winter coat when next fall rolls around, you're in good company.

Money Matters

Buying out-of-season stuff to give as gifts can be a big boost to your wallet or pocketbook, and nobody but you needs to know when you bought them.

Let's face it: It's hard to think winter coat when the daffodils are blooming outside. You're looking forward to the activities that spring brings—not thinking about being warm next winter. But think about how smart you'd be to buy the winter coat now. Think how great you'd feel on the first cold morning next fall when you pull it out of the closet and put it on. Think what you could do with the money you'd save by buying it now. It's not always appealing to buy out-of-season merchandise, but it can save you significant dollars.

Figuring Out Where to Buy

Now that we've covered how to buy, it's important to think about where you'll spend your money. There never have been more opportunities for buying than there are today. You can take the traditional route and head over to the mall, or you can visit one of the increasing number of specialty shops that are popping up. You can shop by catalogue and never even have to get dressed, or you can join the hordes of people who have taken to shopping online. In this section, we check out some of the advantages and disadvantages of different means of shopping and examine where you might get the most for your money.

Department Stores

Department stores such as Macy's, Dillard's, Lord & Taylor, Bloomingdale's, Robinson's-May, Foley's, or Kaufmann's, are great. They carry a variety of items—clothing, gifts, cosmetics, housewares, and stuff for kids—and they generally have pretty good service. You can return items (as long as you save your receipt) if you decide you don't want them or have problems with them. You can go and look at what you're thinking about buying, or try on clothing to see how you'll look in it.

When shopping in a department store, be sure to consider sales events. That pair of pants you like that costs $43 today might be on sale this very weekend for $29.99. That new bedspread you saw for your room might be marked down 50 percent during the store's big sale at the end of the month. Many salespeople know, and are happy to tell you, if the item you're thinking about buying will be on sale in the near future.

Specialty Shops

Specialty shops are fun, but they're generally more expensive than department or discount stores. Specialty shops are where you'll find funky stuff that doesn't show up in more mainstream stores. If that sort of merchandise appeals to you, you might do well in these kinds of store. As with department stores, be sure to check out the possibility of upcoming sales, or look for off-season merchandise.

Imagine That

Specialty shops often are small and locally owned. If you're brave, you can ask the owner to give you a price break on an item you really like. He or she might be willing to take a little less profit to move the item. Can't hurt to ask, right?

Discount Stores

Popular with many people, discount stores offer a variety of merchandise, typically at lower prices than traditional department stores. There are different kinds of discount stores, and prices among them will vary.

The big discount marts such as Ames and Wal-Mart can offer low prices because they buy merchandise in huge quantities. They might offer some of the same brands you'll find in department stores, but generally the merchandise is not as high-end as you'll find at Macy's or Dillard's. Other discount places offer merchandise that's slightly flawed, or that's from a close-out lot, or left over from the previous year. These kinds of places include T.J. Maxx and Filene's Basement, and stores that vary locally that offer everything from beauty and health care items to discontinued wallpaper and ceramic tile.

Discount stores are becoming more and more prevalent, and offer some good bargains. Some of them also offer some good junk, so be careful.

Money Matters

Save big on shampoo, makeup, and related items in stores that buy merchandise that has been discontinued or buy from stores that go out of business. You might find a bottle of Herbal Essence for less than half the price that you'd pay at the drug store.

Outlet Stores

Outlet stores cropped up for a while across the country like Christmas lights do after Thanksgiving. Many of them were included in outlet "malls," which put various shops together in one complex. For whatever reasons, many of these outlet complexes failed and were shut down.

There are, however, many outlet stores still around, and they do offer some good shopping values. As with discount stores, outlets might offer merchandise that's less than perfect, or that's left over from a previous season.

Some outlets, such as the VF Factory Outlet in Wyomissing, PA, offer all merchandise at 50 percent or more off the regular retail price. The VF Corp. owns companies such as Lee (think jeans), Jansport (think backpacks), Joe Boxer (think jammies), Wrangler, Jantzen, Healthtex, and more. One of the original outlet centers in the country, it truly is a manufacturer's outlet, and you can find great buys there.

However, beware of the outlets that are really nothing more than places to sell merchandise that nobody wanted when it was for sale at department or discount stores.

Scary Stuff

Be sure to check out return policies when you're shopping at a discount or outlet store, and examine the merchandise carefully before you buy. It's no bargain to end up with damaged merchandise that can't be returned.

On the Net

There's no question about it, Internet shopping is hot. It's estimated that Americans spent about $20 billion on e-commerce in 2000, most of which was attributed to online catalog sales. This e-shopping boom is causing nearly everyone to want a piece of the action. Department stores such as Nordstrom's and Dillard's are selling online. So are Kmart and Wal-Mart. There's online outlet shopping, fine shopping, one-of-a-kind shopping, and of course, auction shopping.

You can buy Belgian chocolates, Holland tulips, Scottish salmon, and French films with a few clicks of the mouse. You can buy golf equipment, clothing, gifts, food, exotic pets, and nearly every kind of household item available online.

Experts predict that Internet shopping will continue to increase as consumers grow more accustomed to the idea and come to understand the many advantages of online shopping. Nearly any material item you might want probably can be found somewhere on the Internet. The selection and variety is incredible, and there are bargains if you know where to look.

Follow these guidelines when shopping online to assure that your experience will be a good one:

✧ Make sure the site on which you're shopping is secure. A secured site seals your personal information—including your credit card number—so that nobody can get access to it. Read the site's privacy statement before you begin shopping.

✧ Print out the receipt and the confirmation of sale that you get online. These serve as records of your transaction, and you might need them later.

✧ When your credit card bill arrives, be sure to compare the amount you were charged with that on the receipt you printed out. Discrepancies have been known to occur.

✧ Record the customer service number that shows up when you order something on the Internet. Write it down on the receipt you print out. That will make it easy to reference your purchase should a problem occur.

✧ Write down the Internet address of the sites from which you order merchandise, or include them in your listing of favorite sites. This will make it easier to find them if you have a problem or want to shop there again.

There's tons of competition among online retailers, so many are looking to give you a bargain to get you to their site. You'll sometimes see notices of special deals when you log on to the Internet, or you can look for deals at sites such as www.mycoupons.com.

The biggest danger of shopping online isn't the remote possibility of somebody getting hold of your credit card number or your items not showing up after you order them. Because of the sheer vastness of stuff out there, it's really easy to get carried away. If you're thinking of buying on the Web, it's a good idea to set a limit of what you'll spend. That way you can shop for as long as you'd like, but you'll only spend within your limit.

Mail Order

Mail-order shopping is still popular, even though many of the catalogs now are available online. There are discount mail order companies, but many of them are pricey. The good thing, however, is that like department stores, many catalogue companies offer great prices on items that are overstocks or out of season. Don't forget to look for these bargains.

However you decide to shop, don't spend more money than you'll be able to pay off at the end of the month unless it's a major item for which you've planned.

Some Things Are Better the Second Time Around

When you're looking to get the most for your money, don't overlook the possibility of buying secondhand. Many, many apartments have been furnished with secondhand stuff. Secondhand stores sometimes turn up some funky, retro clothing and other items for cheap, cheap, cheap.

Get online to find just about anything you can imagine that somebody is trying to get rid of—computers, sports equipment, or musical instruments. You name it, and it's probably for sale someplace on the Internet.

The danger, of course, is that it's more difficult to know what you're getting when you buy secondhand. Be especially wary of electronic equipment or anything else that costs a significant amount of money. If, whether you're buying online or person to person, the seller seems in a big hurry to get rid of something, or won't let you test out the item before you buy, it's probably best to let it go.

Shops that sell furniture, electronics, musical instruments, sports equipment, and other secondhand items should be willing to give you a receipt when you buy. Be sure to ask about a return policy before you hand over your cash.

It's important to get the most for your money, regardless of what or how much you're buying. Regardless of how much money you have or expect to have someday, it's smart to spend carefully.

Check out the Teenagers Today Web site for all kinds of tips and opportunities for saving money when shopping online. You'll find it at http://teenagerstoday.com.

The Least You Need to Know

✧ It's important to make the most of your money, no matter how much—or little—you have.

✧ There are circumstances under which it's fine to buy, but waiting for a while to make a purchase often is better.

✧ Gauging the right time to buy often is as important as what you buy.

✧ There are a multitude of shopping opportunities, ranging from the dependable old department stores to the Internet.

✧ Knowing the best place to shop for the different things you want can add up to significant savings.

✧ Buying secondhand can be smart, but be sure to know what you're getting.

Chapter 12

The Wheels Thing

In This Chapter

✧ Understanding why we love our cars

✧ Deciding if, and when, to buy your first car

✧ Negotiating different options for buying a car

✧ Exploring some alternatives to car ownership

✧ Keeping routine car expenses in mind

Probably one of the first major purchases you'll make during your lifetime, or that someone will make for you, is a car. The phrase "I can't wait until I have a car of my own" is a common theme among teens who see a set of wheels as a means of independence and a sign of maturity, as well as a convenient method of getting from one place to another.

Our society depends on automobiles for convenience and speed. We don't like to have to wait for a bus or train, or to depend on someone else for transportation. We like to step out to our garage or the curb, get into our cars, and take off. That's not to say, however, that cars are really necessary for everyone. We talked about the difference between wanting something and really needing it in Chapter 2, "Using Money to Get What You Want" and that discussion certainly applies to cars. There are families in America that own more cars than there are family members.

In this chapter, we look at how Americans became so car crazy in the first place, and the implications of owning a car. You also learn about good and not-so-good ways of buying a car, in case you and your parents decide there's one in your future. And because this book is about your money and finances, you've got to know about all the expenses involved with owning a car. So, put up your feet and let's talk cars.

America's Love Affair with the Automobile

There's no question about it, Americans love their cars. We bought more new cars and trucks in 1999 than in any other year—nearly 17 million of them. That's not to say that we didn't buy a lot of cars before the end of the 20th century. Organized in 1903, the Ford Motor Company had sold more than a million cars by 1920 (remember there were a lot fewer people back then). The automobile has had, and continues to have, a huge impact on the way we live.

Imagine That

Almost half of the total automobile sales in 1999 were trucks or sport utility vehicles (SUVs)—an indication that we not only want cars, we want big, powerful machines that will take us anyplace, even if we just use them to drive the kids to school and go to the grocery store.

Automobiles give us great freedom. They give us the freedom to work in a town that we live miles away from, visit friends and family whenever we want to, and travel to places we might not otherwise see. Consider that, years ago, the practical limit of wagon travel in a day was 10 to 15 miles. That means that anyone who lived farther than that from a city, a railroad, or a form of water transportation was virtually isolated. Can you imagine being able to go no farther than 15 miles in a day? It's practically unthinkable to a nation of people who hop into cars and drive that distance to go for dinner at a restaurant we like.

Imagine That

It's been said that Henry Ford freed common people from the limits of their geography when he marketed the first car produced for mass consumption. Gotta agree with that!

Think for a minute about all the businesses and industries related to our automobiles. In addition to the companies that actually manufacture cars, there are loads of businesses that wouldn't exist if there were no cars. Consider those listed in the following:

- ✧ Fuel stations
- ✧ Auto repair shops
- ✧ Drive-through restaurants, banks, and so forth
- ✧ Highway construction firms
- ✧ Highway patrol and police
- ✧ Convenience stores
- ✧ Car washes

✧ Accessories for cars such as seat covers, fancy hubcaps, and those auto deodorizer trees

✧ Car insurance companies

✧ Licensing centers

✧ Car radio system manufacturers

An interesting thing is that many Americans strongly identify with the cars they drive. In some ways, our cars become extensions of who we are. Many people display bumper stickers on their cars or decorate them in other ways to personalize them. You probably know at least one or two people who spend inordinate amounts of time cleaning, polishing, and waxing their cars. We also tend to admire people, at least superficially, who drive the newest, fastest, fanciest cars. How many times have you heard somebody say something like, "Oh, you know Charlie. He's the guy with the Porsche"?

To some degree, we even expect people to buy cars that fit their status and station in life. You'd probably look twice if you saw the governor of your state cruising through town in a beat-up, rusty, old Ford Escort. That's because someone who's been assigned a level of public status and authority is expected to have a car that fits that persona.

Imagine That

People in the United States, on average, own twice as many cars and drive twice as many miles each year as their parents did during the 1950s, according to Alan Durning, the author of *Asking How Much Is Enough*.

Is There a Car in Your Future?

Having said all that, let's get back to you and cars. Is there a car in your life anytime soon? Maybe you've already decided that you're ready to get a car. Hopefully, your parents agree with you and everyone has the same expectations. Maybe you're thinking you'd like to get a car within the next two or three years. Maybe you already have a car. Maybe you (or your parents) have decided that you really don't need a car, and you're happily (or not) left riding your bike, catching a lift, walking, or rollerblading when you need to get some-place.

We've already established that cars aren't for everybody. Most teens who live in New York or another major city aren't like-ly to need cars because they can walk or catch a bus, subway, or taxi to wherever they're going. Besides, it's very expensive to park a car in a big city, making it infeasible for many peo-ple.

If you have decided you'll get a car—either right away, or down the road (no pun intended)—there are some important questions to think about:

✧ When will you get it?

✧ How will you pay for it?

✧ How will you pay to maintain it after you get it?

✧ What rules will apply to you having the car?

As you know, cars are expensive. They're expensive to acquire and expensive to keep once you get them. You'll read about costs associated with keeping a car later in the chapter. For now, let's assume that you're ready to buy a car and have a look at what might be the best way for you to do so.

Buying an Automobile

If you're ready to buy a car, you can take one of two general approaches. You can either decide exactly what kind of car you want and then go about finding that particular vehicle or start looking around to see what's available and then decide what car you want.

Some teens are lucky. Their parents choose and buy a car for them. If your parents are willing to do that, count your blessings. Hopefully, they'll get something you like and not a 1989 Plymouth station wagon with wood panels. Even so, some people think that any car is better than no car.

What Will It Cost to Buy a Car?

If you've decided on what kind of car you want and you're going out to price new cars, or you're going out to price used ones to get an idea of what's available, prepare yourself. Sticker shock is alive and well in your local car dealerships. Let's have a look at what some new cars are listed for. Remember that prices will vary depending on where you live and the availability of the vehicle.

At the time of this writing, the car ads in my area show that a 2001 GMC Jimmy 4x4 goes for $26,350. A 2001 Suzuki Grand Vitara 4x4 is value priced at $18,295. A 2001 C240 Mercedes-Benz (hey, it doesn't hurt to look, and besides, the C Class models are at the low end of the Mercedes price range) is on sale for $37,660.

Money Matters

If you buy a used car privately, it's a good idea to take it to a reputable, neutral mechanic and have it thoroughly checked over. This will cost you some money, but is much better than buying a lemon and having huge repair bills later. Also, be sure to get the car's maintenance record.

Of course, there are new cars for less money. A 2001 Kia Rio is priced at $7,995. Of course, it's *really* small. A 2001 Toyota Corolla (that's *not* a Camry) is marked at $12,995. A 2001 Nissan Sentra GXE costs $13,790. Of course, it looks like something your mom would drive.

Granted, these are brand-new cars, just coming onto the lot for a new year. Maybe it would make sense to look at some of the leftover 2000 models, right? They'd probably cost a lot less than the brand-new cars. Fasten your seat belt. You're in for more sticker shock.

A 2000 leftover model of one of those cute little VW Beetles that everybody likes will run you $21,050. A 2000 Jetta is priced at $19,450, and a 2000 Passat at $23,770. A Toyota Camry 2000 leftover is available for $18,242. A 2000 Volvo sedan that was used as a demo model can be had for $28,888. Consider these less expensive 2000 models: A Ford Focus is priced at $12,450, a Ford Ranger at $11,950, and a Kia Sephia at $8,005.

If the 2000 bargains still sound like a lot of money, you might want to think about buying a used car. There are a lot of low-mileage cars around that have been well cared for, and if you buy a used car from a reputable dealer, you might get a limited warranty with it to protect you in case of trouble later. The Federal Trade Commission's Used Car Rule requires dealers to post a buyer's guide in every used car they offer for sale. The guide will tell you whether the car comes with a warranty and gives a lot of other information as well.

Are good, used cars really that cheap, though? Let's look at what some in the Reading, Pennsylvania area were selling for in December 2000: A two-year-old Isuzu Rodeo SE 4x4 was listed for $18,995. A year-old Mazda Miata sport convertible cost $17,995, a year-old Jeep Wrangler sport convertible was $18,995, and a two-year-old VW Beetle was $14,990.

All of those are fairly new cars, so you could consider buying an older model. Just remember those cars probably will have higher mileage, and you're more likely to run into problems than with a newer car. Let's see what some cars five years or older were listed for: A 1995 Isuzu Rodeo with 80,000 miles on it will still cost $9,990. A 1993 Ford Taurus with 72,000 miles was listed at $6,950. A 1994 Oldsmobile Cutlass Supreme with 59,000 miles cost $8,995. A 1994 Jeep Grand Cherokee with 78,000 was listed at $12,495.

Scary Stuff

Unless you know a lot about repairing cars, resist the temptation to buy an old junker because you can get it for a great price. If you give in to that temptation, you're likely to end up paying for the car many times over just to keep it running.

There you have it. New cars are expensive. Leftover new cars from the previous year are expensive. Fairly new used cars are expensive. Even not-so-new, used cars with high mileage can be expensive. Still, you want a car.

Financing Your Car

If you don't have somebody buying the car for you and you don't have enough money to buy it yourself, you'll have to think about financing the purchase over time. If you're not at least 18 with a credit history and a regular income, you'll probably need a parent or other qualified adult to sign for the loan, or to co-sign for it with you. If you're considering financing a car, keep the following tips in mind:

✧ Get a loan from a bank or credit union instead of from a car dealership. Dealer financing normally costs at least one or two percentage points more than a bank.

Scary Stuff

Beware of finance companies that guarantee loans to any-one, regardless of credit problems, income, or past histories. These companies are taking a risk with their money, and they usually charge higher interest rates on their loans than a bank or credit union.

✧ Be realistic about the loan you request. Don't ask for more than you'll be able to comfortably pay back.

✧ Put down as much money on the car as you can. The more you pay up front, the lower your interest rate will be. Plus, you'll be financing less and paying less overall.

✧ If you're buying a new car that offers a rebate (that's money the car manufacturer offers you as an incentive to buy its product), use the rebate as part of your down payment.

✧ Get the shortest-term loan that you can manage. Don't make car payments for seven years if you can pay the loan off in three. You'll end up paying interest for a longer period of time, which means you'll pay more in-terest.

✧ Interest on a car loan isn't tax-deductible, but interest on a home equity loan is. If the loan is in your parents' name and they own a house, they might want to con-sider making it a home equity instead of a car loan.

✧ If you come into some extra money, maybe for your high school graduation or a birthday, put it toward the loan and get it paid off early, if possible. Make sure your lender will allow you to do this before you sign for the loan. Some lenders penalize for early payment.

✧ Be sure you understand the terms of the loan before you (or your parents) sign for it. Try to get a simple interest loan instead of an installment loan. A simple interest loan lets you pay interest only on the money you still owe on your loan. A front-end installment loan, however, requires you to pay interest on the entire loan, even after you've paid some of it back. If you borrow $6,000 and pay $4,000 back, you'd still be paying interest on $6,000—even though you only owe $2,000.

Leasing a Vehicle

Another option for buying a car that's been gaining in popularity over the past several years is leasing. Again, depending on your age and circumstances, this is something that might have to be done through your parents.

Leasing simply means that you pay a specified amount of money for a specified period of time in exchange for the use of a product—in this case, a car. It's sort of like renting it. Depending on the type of lease agreement you have, you either turn the car back over to the dealer at the end of the period or you can buy it for whatever it's determined to be worth at that point.

Money Matters

For more information on leasing a vehicle, go online to the Car Buying and Leasing Center at www.leasinghelpline.com. Also check out Lease Guide.com at www.leaseguide.com.

Leasing a vehicle is a controversial topic. Some people swear by it; others just don't get it. Leasing seems to appeal to people who like to have a new car every couple of years, and who like to drive cars they can't afford to buy outright. Many businesses lease cars for their employees. We're not going to spend much more time on leasing a car, but the following are some pros and cons for you to consider.

Good Things:

✧ Many lease agreements require no down payment, or just a very small payment.

✧ You don't have to worry about selling your car when your lease ends. You just give it back.

✧ You probably can lease a more expensive car than you could buy.

Not-So-Good Things:

✧ The total cost of leasing almost always is more expensive than buying a car with cash, and usually more than financing a car.

✧ Most lease agreements limit the number of miles you can drive (usually 15,000 a year), and charge you a steep penalty if you exceed that number.

✧ Leasing doesn't cover car repairs or insurance, so you don't save money in those areas.

✧ When your lease ends, you've got to figure out what to do about a car all over again.

Buying a Car Online

Car buying recently has been launched into a brave new world—the Internet. Buying a car online varies, depending on the site you use to do it. And there are lots and lots of sites out there offering new cars, used cars, vintage cars, trucks, SUVs—you name it.

A big word of caution before we go through the basics of buying online—be careful! Remember that many things (especially people) can be misrepresented on the Internet. Always have an adult with you if you're planning on making a large-scale purchase online. If you're thinking of buying a used car online, be sure you get the terms of the agreement—and never reveal personal information unless you're absolutely certain the seller is legitimate.

Scary Stuff

Teens are famous for their fearless navigation of the Internet, but you need to remember that the Web is an easy place for people with questionable motives to hang out. Don't ever give your name, credit card number, phone number, or address to anyone on the Internet unless you're sure it's a legitimate person or firm.

On a site called CarsDirect.com, online car buying works like this: Using the site's descriptions and images, you pick out exactly the car you want, including colors and options. You'll be given a firm price for what the car will cost. If you agree to the price, you agree to buy, and leave a deposit on your credit card. The CarsDirect.com buying service will find you the exact car you want through its network of dealers. Then you can go pick up the car or arrange to have it delivered to your house.

Some people say they like the idea of buying online because it eliminates the hassle of dealing with car salespeople and haggling over price. Remember, though, that you still need to go to a dealer to test drive a car (most people don't buy cars without testing them first), and there's still some paperwork that has to be done by fax machine.

Buying a car, however you do it, is a big commitment. Maybe it's worth taking just a quick look at other means of getting around town.

Money Matters

Check out Yahoo's car site for a lot more information on car buying online. You'll find it at http://autos.yahoo.com.

Alternatives to Buying a Car

If you live in an area with good public transportation, don't overlook it as an option. Many people use their time on a bus or train to read, write letters (at least I've heard that some people still do that), or catch up on the daily news. Using public transportation might seem like a hassle if you're not used to it, but it really is a feasible option for around-town travel.

Going out of town, on the other hand, can be a different story. I've spent plenty of time on Greyhound buses, and although economical, those rides sure can be … interesting. You just never know who will decide to sit down in that seat next to you.

Bicycles and foot power also are a good means of local transportation. When it's all said and done, however, chances are you still want a car. Okay, okay. I'd be remiss, however, if I didn't fill you in on the expenses involved with owning a car once you have one.

Other Expenses When You Own a Car

Whew! You've just breathed a big sigh of relief because you
finally have your own car. You're so excited that you want to
take it out and show it to all your friends. But what's that
your mom's saying about not driving it until the insurance
deal is final? Come to think of it, you couldn't drive it anyway, because there's no gas in the tank. And was that a little
pinging noise you heard on the way home? Buying a car is
just the start of the expenses involved with car ownership.
Let's have a look at what else you'll be facing.

Gas and Maintenance

With gas prices flirting with $2 a gallon, and more than that
in some areas, gas and maintenance costs are something to
consider. A $20 bill doesn't go too far at the gas pumps these
days, and unless we start digging up Alaska for oil, as some
politicians and businesses have proposed, those prices probably aren't going to go down too much anytime soon.

Imagine That

Even though our gas prices have gotten high, they're still
very low compared to other Western countries. A friend
living in London reported recently that it cost $60 to fill
his car tank, and the car was a Volkswagen Golf!

Unless the manufacturer specifically recommends it, don't
upgrade your gas to premium. Studies have shown that the
regular grade is fine for most cars. Also, get the best gas
mileage possible by keeping filters clean and driving at, or
slower than, the posted speed limit.

Car repairs are expensive, so do the best you can to avoid them by taking good care of your car. Keep up with scheduled maintenance—and don't forget to change your oil! A place such as Jiffy Lube is great for that kind of maintenance because it will check your fluid levels, filters, and so forth.

Insurance

Insurance can be expensive, but you've absolutely got to have it. Even if your state doesn't require it, the liability risk if you're in an accident is simply too great to ignore. If you're under a certain age, you probably can be included on your parents' insurance plan. Ask a parent to discuss the matter with his or her agent. Remind Mom and Dad that insurance rates vary from company to company, so it might be a good idea to shop around if their rates seem high. Also, remember that the best way to keep insurance rates down is to keep your driving record in great shape. That means no accidents, no speeding tickets, and no other violations.

Other Costs

Parking fees, tolls, car wax, car washes, the cost of getting your license and owner's card renewed—all these little things add up over the life of your car. A car can be a real drain on your wallet, so be smart when you're using it to save costs when you can. For instance, if you have to park in a metered space, be sure to put the money in the meter and don't let it run out of time. It's a lot more economical to put two quarters in a meter than to pay a $10 parking fine later.

Wash the car yourself instead of driving it through the deluxe $8 car wash. Think about carpooling to save costs. And remember that your car is a big investment and take care of it. With care and proper maintenance, it should last you until you've saved enough money to buy another one.

We live in the country of cars, and chances are good that sooner or later, you will own one. Preparing ahead to buy a vehicle, and being aware of all the costs associated with owning one, will help your venture into becoming a car owner a little smoother.

The Least You Need to Know

✧ Americans have been in love with their cars since they were first mass-produced in the 1920s.

✧ Not everyone needs a car, but it's a rare teenager who doesn't want one.

✧ Cars are expensive, so think carefully about whether a new or used one makes more sense.

✧ If you don't have cash to pay for a car, you can look into financing or leasing a vehicle.

✧ Buying cars online is catching on, but is not without risks.

✧ Car costs continue even after you have the vehicle by way of insurance, fuel, repairs, maintenance, and so forth.

Part 5

Keeping Track of What You've Got

Once you've got some money, what do you do with it? Do you stash it in a box on the dresser or in a savings account, never to see it again? Of course not. You'll need at least some of the money you have to keep up with your expenses and to buy some of the things you want. To be able to do that, you need to know how to keep track of your money.

It often doesn't make sense to carry around a lot of cash to pay for purchases. That being the case, you might want to think about opening a checking account, or getting a debit card, or both.

Just as with savings accounts, there are different kinds of checking accounts, and some will make more sense for you and your money than others. You learn all about how to choose a checking account in this part, as well as the advantages and potential pitfalls of debit cards and automated teller machines.

Chapter 13

The Great Balancing Act

In This Chapter

✧ Deciding whether you need a checking account

✧ Understanding different types of checking accounts

✧ Determining your banking needs

✧ Choosing the account that makes sense for you

✧ Keeping track of your checking account

Now that you've learned about saving and spending money, it's time to consider how you'll keep track of what you have. When you were a little kid it was easy to keep track of your money. You probably kept it in a bank in your room and took out what you needed when you wanted to buy something. Now that you (presumably) have more money than you used to it doesn't make sense to keep all of it on top of your dresser or stashed in a drawer.

You might have (hopefully) opened a savings account, or maybe you're thinking of opening one. Perhaps you've even looked into setting up a money market account or a certificate of deposit. Those are great vehicles for safekeeping of money that you don't need access to and they allow you to earn interest on that money. What do you do, however, with money that you need to have available to use when you want it?

An alternative to keeping the money in a box on your dresser is to open a checking account. In this chapter, we learn about different kinds of checking accounts, why you might need one, and how to use an account once you have it. Maintaining and using a checking account isn't difficult, but it does require some time and attention.

Americans started using checks one year after the National Banking Act of 1864 established the dollar as the national currency, and we never looked back. Nowadays, Americans write more than 65 billion—that's billion—checks each year, and the number increases annually. Let's look first at who needs a checking account, and find out if one might be right for you.

Knowing When You Need a Checking Account

If you have expenses for which it's not convenient—or not smart—to use cash, you probably would benefit from a checking account. You'll run into more and more occasions as you get older in which writing a check is the only way to go. You probably can still pretty much get away with using cash at this point, but it's not always a good idea.

For instance, you shouldn't send cash through the mail; it's just not a smart thing to do. Envelopes get ripped or unsealed. Stuff falls out of envelopes. If you pay for something with cash, you have no record or proof of payment like you do when you write a check or use a money order. For those reasons, it doesn't make sense to use cash to pay bills by mail, or to pay for items you buy from catalogs, or to send cash through the mail for any reason.

If you owe $96 at Macy's for your back-to-school shopping spree, and you don't want to send cash in the mail, you could take it to the store and pay your bill. Again, however, it doesn't make sense to walk through the mall with almost $100 in your purse or pocket. Purses get stolen or lost and people carrying almost $100 sometimes see something on their way to Macy's bill department that they decide they simply can't live without. So, the best way to pay your Macy's (or whatever) bill is to write a check that you can either mail or deliver to the store.

A checking account is a bank account in which you keep money that you want to be accessible. Your money sits in the account until you write a check in the amount that you need. When you write the check, the money is deducted from your account.

Money Matters

Writing a check is a lot like paying for something with a debit card: Both cause money to be deducted from your checking account.

Let's say you have $100 in your checking account and you just got a notice that you owe $15 for your school yearbook. The notice says that no cash will be accepted and that checks should be made payable to your school. When you write out a check to your school (that's making a check payable to), the amount of the check—in this case $15—will be deducted from the $100 in your checking account.

There are some real advantages to using checks instead of cash.

Not all teens need to have checking accounts, but if you get bills in your name or are responsible for paying for expenses that crop up at school or otherwise, it's probably a good idea to have one. If you think that having a checking account might be a good idea for yourself, read on. If you don't think you need one now, read on anyway—you can keep the information in mind for later.

Finding a Checking Account That's Right for You

It's important to remember that there are big differences among checking accounts. Not all accounts are created equal, and you need to know what you're getting into before you agree to open a particular account.

Money Matters

For all kinds of information relating to banks, banking, and other money topics go to Bankrate.com, found at www. bankrate.com

To get an idea of what's out there, you're going to need to do some shopping. You see, there are various kinds of checking accounts. There are …

✧ Interest-bearing accounts

✧ Non-interest-bearing accounts

✧ Joint accounts

✧ Senior or student accounts

✧ Lifeline accounts

✧ Express accounts

When you're considering opening a checking account, the first thing you need to do is think about how you'll use it. You probably won't be writing many checks unless you have special circumstances. Try to estimate about how many checks you'll write each month.

If for some reason you write a lot of checks, you need to consider that when you shop for the right account. Some checking accounts carry a fee for every check you write. If you write a lot of checks, an account with a fee for every check you write doesn't make sense for you. However, if you'll be writing only two or three checks each month, that kind of account might be right for you because it might have lower overall fees that would make up for the cost of writing checks. Let's look at some different kinds of checking accounts.

Interest-Bearing Accounts

Interest-bearing accounts are great, if you can find them. However, they usually require a minimum balance to open, and you probably need to maintain a minimum balance to avoid fees.

Some interest-bearing accounts pay a flat interest rate, but others vary the rate depending on your account balance—the higher the balance, the more interest you earn. Still, the average interest rate on checking accounts is low—less than 2 percent.

Imagine That

The average interest rate on checking accounts is 1.52 percent, according to Bankrate.com. Better than nothing, but not much to get excited about.

Some banks give you interest on your checking account if you also have a savings account in which you maintain a minimum (usually pretty high) balance. If you can find a no-strings-attached, interest-bearing checking account, go for it. But, be sure you ask a lot of questions and make sure you have all the information concerning any account before you sign on the dotted line.

Non-Interest Bearing Accounts

A non-interest-bearing account, obviously, does not pay you any interest on the money you have in it, but if you can find a free checking account or a low-fee account, you might be better off in the long run. Most teenagers don't have enough money in their checking accounts to earn a lot of interest. It's a better trade-off to give up interest in exchange for not getting socked with a lot of bank fees.

Non-interest-bearing accounts sometimes are called basic checking accounts, and are intended for customers who don't maintain high balances. Some basic accounts require that you maintain a low minimum balance to avoid fees.

Scary Stuff

There are advantages to joint checking accounts, but there can be a downside as well. If one person writes a check (especially a big one) and forgets to tell the other, chances for an overdrawn account increase. If you ever have a joint account, be meticulous about your record keeping.

Joint Checking Accounts

A joint account is one that's owned by two or more people who share equal access to the money in it. It's usually used by people who live together and share household expenses. Each person's name appears on the checks.

Checking accounts aren't the only bank accounts that can be joint accounts. Savings and money market accounts also can be in more than one person's name.

Senior or Student Checking Accounts

Many banks and credit unions offer special deals for students and senior citizens. Be sure to ask about this when you're shopping for your checking account. You might be eligible for free checking, free ATM use, and even more.

Lifeline Checking Accounts

Lifeline checking accounts are for low-income customers. They don't offer a lot of extras, but fees are very low (usually from nothing to $6 a month), and usually they don't require a minimum balance. Some states require that banks offer these types of accounts and even set the terms and conditions for them.

Express Checking Accounts

Express checking accounts are specially designed for people who would rather do their banking electronically or by phone, rather than dealing face to face with a teller. Express accounts usually have low or no monthly fees, no limit on the number of checks you can write, and low minimum balance requirements. You should know, however, that if you open this type of account and then for whatever reasons need the services of a bank teller, you'll pay for those services. Some banks charge $3 or more for express customers to see a teller.

Now that you know a little about different kinds of accounts, how do you go about picking the one that might be right for you? In the next section, we'll provide a whole list of questions you should ask at each bank while you're shopping for the best checking account. Then you can compile your information and see which account makes the most sense for you.

Questions to Ask When Shopping for a Checking Account

There are lots of questions you should ask when considering a particular checking account and you've got to be willing to take a little time to do so. If a bank employee isn't willing to spend some time with you to answer your questions, either in person or by phone, you don't want to be a customer at that bank.

Money Matters

If you're treated rudely by a bank employee, get on the phone and report the incident to the manager. Tell whomever answers the phone that you have a complaint and would like to speak to the appropriate person. Be sure that you're polite and respectful, but don't let the matter go unnoticed.

Some things to ask about include the following:

✧ How much money do I need to open the account?

✧ Does the account pay interest?

✧ Do you have special accounts for students?

✧ Is there a monthly service charge on the account?

✧ Must I maintain a minimum balance to avoid fees?

✧ Is there a limit on the number of checks I can write each month?

✧ How much will it cost to order new checks?

✧ What is the fee for an overdrawn account?

✧ Does the bank offer overdraft protection?

✧ Is there a fee for overdraft protection?

✧ Will I get the checks I write returned with my monthly statement?

✧ How many days between the time I deposit money in my checking account and the time I can write checks on that money?

✧ Can I check my account balances and account history by telephone or computer?

✧ Is there a fee for me to check my account balances or get my account history?

✧ Are checking fees waived if I keep a minimum balance in a savings account in the same bank?

I know that this sounds like a lot to find out from every bank you talk to. However, it's worth taking the time to do because checking accounts vary so much from one bank to another.

As you talk to bank employees take notes to keep all the information sorted out. Don't be afraid to take your time to get all the information you need. You're a potential customer and should be important to the bank.

Money Matters

It sounds like an obvious matter, but consider the location of the bank you'll be dealing with before choosing a checking account. Will it be convenient for you? Will you be able to get there?

How to Write a Check

Writing a check is easy, because each check tells you what you need to include. Let's look at the information you need to include when you write a check:

✧ **The complete and accurate name of the person or company to which you're writing the check.** Don't use nicknames, and be sure you have the complete and correct name for stores, catalogue services, or whatever.

✧ **The correct date.** Don't try to fool your bank by putting a later date on a check because you're not sure you have money to cover it. Make sure the date you use is correct.

✧ **The amount of the check in numbers.** Make sure you start writing the numbers close to the printed dollar sign. Writing the amount so that it looks like this: $ 130.00 gives opportunity for an unscrupulous person to slip in an extra number or two.

✧ **The amount of the check in words.** Start as far to the left of the line as possible to give yourself room. If there's room left over to the right of the line, fill in the rest of the space with a wavy line.

✧ **Your full signature.** This should be signed as it appears on the signature card you filled out when you opened the account.

✧ **A memo.** Use this line to write any notes or information you think you might need concerning the check. If you're paying a bill, many companies request that you write your account number on the memo line to help them process your payment more easily.

Keeping Track of Checks You Write

It's not difficult to keep track of the checks you write, but it does require diligence and attention. If you don't keep track of every check you write, you won't know how much money you have in your account and you'll be at risk for bouncing a check. Bouncing a check is what happens when you write a check that's for more money than you have in the account.

Banks really don't like it when customers bounce checks and they often charge hefty fees when it happens—the average is $25 a bounce. Also, even one bounced check can make it difficult to get another checking account.

If you're writing a check and it's inconvenient at that moment to take the time to record it in your checkbook, write the information on another piece of paper and put it someplace where you'll be able to find it later. Just don't forget to write it in your checkbook as soon as possible.

Balancing Your Checkbook

Some people actually enjoy balancing their checkbooks. For others, it's worse than final exams or a blind date with the son or daughter of your mother's old college friend. Regardless of whether or not you like to do it, balancing your checkbook is a job that needs to be done. Trust me on this: Faithfully balancing your account will save you from some very serious hassles.

Keeping Your Balance in Balance

Remember, there's more to consider when balancing your checkbook than just the checks you write. If you have an ATM card (much more about those in Chapter 14, "ATMs and Debit Cards"), those transactions need to be considered. So do any fees your bank has charged you. Don't overlook anything that affects your account. Once you've identified everything that will affect your account, you need to subtract it from your account balance. Don't forget to record any deposits you've made since your last statement, too, and add them to the balance.

Use your bank statement to help you when you're balancing your checkbook, but don't assume that the statement is always 100 percent correct. Banks sometimes make mistakes, you know. If you see something on the statement that doesn't look right, don't hesitate to call your bank to check on it.

Don't Spend That Money Yet!

To really understand and be able to accurately keep track of your checking account and avoid bouncing checks, it's important that you know your bank's check-hold policy. Let's say that Uncle Bob comes through for your birthday with a check for $50. You promptly write him a thank-you note, and then walk down to the bank to deposit the gift in your checking account.

Imagine That

Be on the lookout for new technologies that might make checking a lot easier in the future. E-check transactions eliminate paper checks all together and electronic check presentment combines the use of paper and electronics.

On the way back from the bank, you pass your favorite sports store and notice there's a big sale going on. You go in and, sure enough, that bright-orange Reebok fleece that you've had your eye on for weeks is on sale for only $39.99. Hardly able to believe your luck, you whip out a check and use it to buy the fleece, which you happily wear to walk the rest of the way home.

Things stop looking so good, however, when you find out from your bank that you've been charged $25 because you overdrew your account. If you'd been aware of your bank's check-hold policy, you would have known that it routinely holds checks for two days or more before crediting them to depositors' accounts.

Obviously, this policy can cause a great deal of trouble if you're not aware of it. Banks are permitted to do this, and it's up to customers to read the regulations carefully to learn about it. Checks for very large amounts, or that come from another state, can be held up to eight days. Another thing to consider is that a deposit made after a certain time of day might not be processed until the following day. If you show up Wednesday afternoon at 4:00 P.M. to deposit a check, chances are you might have missed the transaction cutoff for that day, and your deposit won't be processed until Thursday. Understanding these policies can help you to more easily keep track of what's going on with your checking account.

Don't assume that just because you have a checking account you have to use it for everything. Cash is fine—even preferable—for small purchases, and will make balancing your checkbook easier than if you write checks for every little thing you buy.

The Least You Need to Know

✧ Not everybody needs a checking account, but if you're responsible for bills in your name or paying for other items, it's a good thing to consider.

✧ There are different kinds of checking accounts, so you'll have to find the one that best meets your needs.

✧ Don't be afraid to ask a lot of questions when shopping around at different banks for a checking account; and don't be intimidated by bank employees who might be reluctant to take the time to answer those questions.

✧ Taking time to record each transaction that affects your checking account and to balance your checkbook each month will save you lots of trouble in the long run.

✧ You need to understand all of your bank's policies that affect your checking account to balance your checkbook properly.

Chapter 14

ATMs and Debit Cards

In This Chapter

✧ Why banks love ATMs

✧ Understanding ATMs and debit cards

✧ Finding the best ATM

✧ Saving money on ATM fees

✧ Watching for potential pitfalls

Was there really life before automated teller machines (ATMs)? I mean, can you imagine having to actually walk into a bank, write out a withdrawal slip, wait in line, and hand the slip to a teller just to get a few dollars from your checking account?

It probably was before your lifetime, but yes, there was life before ATMs, and it was much as I just described. If you needed money, you could go to the bank and make a withdrawal from an account you had there. You could write a check at the grocery store or another location for more than the cost of your purchase and get some money back. You could borrow money from a friend or family member. However, you couldn't swing by the ATM on your way back from swimming practice and get $20 to go out to dinner with your friends.

In this chapter, we look at the history of ATMs, how they work, and the advantages and disadvantages of these handy machines.

The History of ATMs

Automatic teller machines first showed up about 20 years ago, but they weren't nearly as common or as popular as they are today. In fact, people were mistrustful of the machines, and banks had to run special promotions and offer gimmicks to get people to try them.

Imagine That

Customers might have been reluctant to use ATMs 20 years ago, but today the average person visits a machine 72 times a year. A category of ATM patrons known as heavy users bank at the machines an average of 156 times a year.

Of course, in time people got used to ATMs, and now they're as common as mailboxes or phone booths. In fact, ATMs are everywhere these days. You can find them in grocery stores, restaurants, coffee shops, department stores, movie theaters, convenience stores, and gas stations—wherever you might find yourself needing some cash.

So, why were banks so anxious to push these ATMs? They'll tell you it was to provide more convenient and better service for their customers, but we know differently, don't we?

Money Matters

According to the Center for Responsive Law, banks today make more than $2 billion a year on ATM transactions. Not bad—for the banks, that is!

Banks love ATMs because, unlike human employees, they work 24 hours a day without complaining. And, it costs banks only about 27 cents to have a deposit or withdrawal processed at an ATM, as compared to about $1.07 for a live teller to handle the transaction.

However, the real reason banks love ATMs is that the machines generate huge amounts of money through the fees associated with them. When ATMs were first introduced, there were no fees. You could go to any machine and use its services free of charge. However, as ATMs became more accepted and popular, banks grabbed the opportunity to use them as moneymakers. Now, the majority of ATMs have fees and banks encourage their customers to use them. In fact, some banks will charge customers for making transactions with a teller inside the bank. You can't win!

How Do ATMs Work?

To get cash from an ATM machine, you need three things:

✧ An ATM card

✧ A personal identification number (PIN)

✧ Cash in a checking or savings account in a bank or credit union that's hooked up with the ATM system

Money Matters

If you deposit money in a bank account and try to use an ATM card soon after, your account balance is likely to come up short. That's because your deposit hasn't yet been credited to your account.

You can apply for an ATM card when you open an account at the bank. You might get a card immediately, or you might have to wait until it's processed and mailed to you. Check to see if your bank, thrift, or credit union charges an annual fee for an ATM card. If it does, be sure to ask how much it will cost.

An ATM card is no good if you don't have a PIN to go with it. Your PIN is a secret number that you need to punch into the ATM every time you conduct a transaction. You insert your card into the machine, then enter your PIN, which gives you clearance to do business. If an incorrect PIN is entered more than two or three times, the machine usually will shut down.

You can use most ATM cards to access cash from a checking or savings account, to transfer money from one account to another, and to check account balances. Some ATM machines allow you to make deposits. However, the main purpose of ATMs is to give you access to your cash.

Some ATM cards, called debit cards, also can be used to make purchases in stores, with the amount of the purchase deducted directly from your checking account. There normally is no fee for that service, and you often can get cash back above the cost of your purchase.

Scary Stuff

Be aware that, if you use an ATM machine to check account balances or transfer funds, you might end up paying a separate fee for each transaction. Ouch!

Is One ATM Better Than Another?

Yes. Some ATMs are better than others because they don't charge a fee, or they charge a lower fee, for you to access your money. Normally, machines that your bank owns will not charge you a fee. And, there sometimes are free ATMs in convenience stores or other locations. Using a machine that belongs to a bank other than your own, or a national ATM such as Cirrus or Plus, probably will result in fees—sometimes as high as $3 per transaction.

Money Matters

It's really important to know where the free ATMs are if your account is with a small institution or you bank online. Internet banks and some small banks and credit unions don't have their own machines, forcing you to pay someone else for the ATM privilege if you don't find a free machine.

Needless to say, ATMs that don't charge you to withdraw your own money are better than those that do. Find the ones in your area that either are owned by your bank or are free, and use them whenever possible.

Advantages of ATMs and Debit Cards

The question is, why do people keep on using ATMs if they get hit up with fees all the time? I mean, you can end up spending a lot of money, just to get your money. You know the answer to that question: We use ATMs because they're so darned convenient, and we're willing to pay for that convenience.

ATMs are plentiful, and they're always open. You can drive up to one in your pajamas at 3 a.m. and get money. You can get money on Veteran's Day, New Year's Day, or the Fourth of July—days when you'd be hard pressed to find a bank open anywhere.

Debit cards, as mentioned earlier, also can be used to your advantage. For instance, if you buy a book of stamps at a U.S. Post Office, you can use your debit card to pay for the stamps and ask the postal clerk for $20 extra. The clerk will deduct $26.60 from your checking account—$6.60 for a book of 33-cent stamps, and $20 that you'll take in cash. You also can do this at some other places, such as grocery or drugstores. Not every place offers this service, however, so don't assume that you'll always be able to get extra cash.

Using your debit card to get extra cash when you need it is a smart idea, because you don't pay fees. I shop at a grocery store where I can get up to $50 back (with no fee) when I pay for the groceries with my debit card. Or, I can pay $2.00 to use the same card in the ATM located inside the same store. That's a no-brainer, for sure.

Getting Around ATM Fees

If you use ATMs a lot, chances are you're going to run into some fees—at least some of the time. There are ways, however, to minimize the costs associated with these handy-dandy machines.

Let's first figure out how much ATMs are costing us. Remember the statistic earlier that the average person uses an ATM 72 times a year? If Joe Average averages a $1 fee for each use, he's shelling out $72 a year for the privilege of getting his own money. If he averages a $2 fee at each use, he's up to $144 a year. At $3 a shot, Joe's paying out $216 a year to gain access to his money.

Money Matters

The amount of money you can get back on your debit card varies from business to business. Don't assume you'll be able to get $30 back at your local drugstore, for instance. Its policy might be to give a maximum of only $20 back.

Now, let's think about that heavy user. Jane has a really bad ATM habit. I mean, she's practically a permanent fixture at her neighborhood machine. She's there 156 times a year, and pays $2 at each visit, which means Jane pays $312 in ATM fees each year. If she averages $3 in fees every time she uses the machine, she'll be out $468 at the end of the year. Think about what Jane could have done with the almost $500 in fees that she handed over to the bank.

Let's look at some ways that Joe and Jane could hang on to some of their hard-earned money instead of letting the bank take it as ATM fees:

✧ Use proprietary or free machines whenever it's possible, not just whenever it's convenient.

✧ Don't withdraw money in bits and pieces. If you're going to need $50 for the coming week, withdraw $50 all at once from the ATM. This eliminates the necessity of returning to the ATM and incurring more fees.

✧ Use your debit card whenever possible to get extra cash when you make a purchase.

✧ If your own bank doesn't have a machine that's convenient for you to use, shop around. Don't assume that all machines are the same—the fees vary as much as $2 per transaction.

ATMs are convenient, there's no doubt about it, and with some planning and determination, you should be able to avoid most of the fees associated with their use. Still, there are some troublesome aspects of ATMing.

Scary Stuff

Don't be lulled into assuming a particular ATM doesn't have a fee because it doesn't display a message on the screen while you're banking. Notice of a fee might be posted as a sticker on the machine itself, and not show up on the screen.

Some Pitfalls of Plastic

It's hard to imagine sometimes that a little plastic card can be the source of so much trouble, but, when not used properly or handled carefully, an ATM card can cause you more problems than it's worth.

Cards get lost, stolen, or left in the machine. If any of those things happen to you, contact the card issuer immediately to report the loss. It's also important to keep safety issues in mind as they relate to using an ATM card. ATM customers have been too-frequent targets of burglaries because thieves see them as ready sources of cash. If somebody approaches you at an ATM and demands your money, hand it over. No amount of money is worth risking injury for. If a thief demands your PIN, reveal the number, but report the theft as quickly as possible afterward.

Try to have at least one other person with you when you use an ATM, especially if it's off by itself at the edge of a parking lot someplace. Never use an ATM by yourself at night. Once you've completed your transaction, move away from the ATM. Don't stand there and count your money or balance your checkbook.

The best defense against any kind of crime, including that associated with ATMS, is to be aware of what's going on around you at all times, and to use good common sense.

It Really Is Money

Grabbing cash from an ATM is easy and convenient. So easy and convenient, in fact, that it's tempting to do so often. Using a debit card to pay for purchases is easy, too. For many people, using a card to pay for something doesn't have the same effect as paying with cash does. It's more abstract. It's easy to convince yourself that you're not really spending money if you don't actually hand money over to the person on the other side of the cash register.

Trust me on this: When you use a debit card to pay for something, you're spending money. When you use an ATM to get money from your account, you're going to spend money. It's really important to keep track of what you've got and what you're doing with it. It's easy to get $10 or $20 from the ATM and not think much about it, until all of the sudden you realize you've spent $100 and you don't have enough left to buy a birthday present for your dad.

ATMs and debit cards have some excellent advantages, but also have the potential for heartache. Use good common sense, take advantage of no-fee or low-fee ATMs, and keep track of what you've got.

The Least You Need to Know

✧ Customers were reluctant to use ATMs at first, but their enthusiasm for them quickly grew.

✧ Banks are crazy about ATMs because they generate billions of dollars a year in fees.

✧ To use an ATM machine you need a card, a PIN, and money in an accessible account.

✧ Some machines are better to use than others, and there are ways to reduce the money you have to pay for ATM fees.

✧ ATMs and debit cards are convenient, but you need to keep close track of your money when using them to avoid trouble.

Part 6
Advanced Money

Once you've mastered the basics of savings accounts, checkbooks, debit cards, saving money, spending money, and so forth, you're ready to move on to some more complex matters of money and finances.

Maybe you've already got a credit card or are thinking about getting one. Maybe you've saved up some money, and you're looking for an opportunity to invest it. Perhaps you're interested in joining or starting an investment club, or maybe you're even thinking about starting your own business.

Although these topics are more advanced than others we've covered in this book, they're areas that more and more teens are becoming involved with. Teenagers no longer sit back and let adults handle their finances. They're right in there, buying stock and making other kinds of investments, starting and growing companies, and handling their finances like old pros.

This part deals with some of those more advanced finance-related topics, and helps you to plan your financial future.

Chapter 15

Understanding Credit Cards and Debt

In This Chapter

✦ The history of credit cards and how they work

✦ Some reasons that it's good to have a credit card

✦ Understanding the pitfalls of using credit

✦ Resisting temptation when using your card

✦ Getting a card if you want one

Credit cards are easy. Credit cards are instant gratification. Credit cards can get you what you want—when you want it. No waiting, no saving, no negotiating with Mom or Dad.

Credit cards also can be dangerous. They've been the cause of big trouble for millions of people who have used them improperly. Credit card debt has forced people into bankruptcy or to sell their homes to pay it off. It's torn apart families and even caused people to kill themselves. It's not the cards themselves that are to blame for this kind of trouble, of course, it's the spending habits of the card owners.

In this chapter, we look at the pros and cons of credit cards and how to be smart about using them. First, let's have a quick look at how credit cards came about and how they got to be so wildly popular.

Who Ever Thought of Credit Cards, Anyway?

It should be no surprise to hear the first credit cards were introduced by banks. As you read earlier, credit cards became popular back in the 1960s, when the Bank of America first began issuing them, and people started using them like crazy.

That's not to say that people didn't buy on credit before the 1960s. The practice of buying something today and paying for it tomorrow—or next week or next month—has been going on for years and years. The difference is, buying on credit used to occur directly between the buyer and the seller—there was nobody in the middle.

Imagine That

According to the National Credit Research Foundation, 55 percent of students between the ages of 16 and 22 have a major credit card.

Let's say you wanted to buy the latest Christina Aguilera CD, but you didn't have enough money. You'd go down to your local store—Bob's CDs—and ask if you could get the CD and have the purchase put on your account. Bob would give you the CD, make a note under your name in his book that you owed him $16.95 plus tax, and off you'd go, earphones happily in place as you sang along with Christina. There was no need for a credit card. Bob trusted you to come up with the money and pay him when you got it. If you didn't, you wouldn't get any more CDs (or anything else) from Bob, and he might put a bill collector or some other unpleasant person on your tail.

Credit cards made things more complicated, and you'd have to look pretty hard these days for a store that would let you put a purchase on your account. However, people loved the idea of using a card to make purchases, and they bought everything from furniture to clothing to vacations on credit.

A big difference between the time when credit cards first became popular and now, however, is that in the 1960s almost everybody paid their cards off at the end of the month. Carrying debt was considered unwise and almost something to be ashamed of. People who got credit cards in the 60s had lived through the Great Depression—or their parents had—and they weren't taking any chances by running up debt. Somewhere along the way, though, we lost our collective uneasiness about owing.

Scary Stuff

You can carry a balance on your credit card forever as long as you pay a minimum amount each month, but if you do, you're heading for a big crash. You don't win in the end by continuing to run up debt without paying it off.

It's estimated today that about 70 percent of cardholders carry a balance from one month to another. This is called revolving consumer debt, and it's on the rise. If you carry a balance on your credit card, it means that you don't pay the full amount of what you owe. Let's say you use a credit card to buy $420 worth of stuff during October. When you get your bill, you can do one of two things. You can write a check for $420 and send it back to the card issuer, or you can make a partial payment on the bill. The bank, or whatever lender issued your card, will set a minimum amount that you must pay. That minimum amount could be as little as $15 or $20.

For whatever reasons, many people don't pay off the full balance of their credit card bill every month. They don't have enough money, they want to use the money for something else, or they just don't understand the dangers of running up lots of debt.

So, let's say you decide to pay the minimum amount, and you send $20 to the bank. That leaves more money in your pocket, but there's a catch. You still owe the bank $400, and the bank's not gonna let you have that money for nothing. You'll be charged interest—a lot of interest—on the money you owe. The average interest on credit card debt is around 17 or 18 percent, although there's so much competition among credit card companies these days that it's starting to drop off a bit.

Money Matters

If you have a credit card that's charging you 16 to 18 percent interest, try looking around for a better rate. Check out Ram Research Card Trak at www.cardtrak.com for a list of cards and rates.

People get into real trouble when they make only the minimum payment and then go out and charge another $420 the next month. If you do that, you'll owe $820 by the time your next bill shows up, plus the interest on the money you hadn't paid last month. Before long, you'll be over your head in credit card debt. However, not everybody runs into trouble with credit cards, and there are some great reasons to have one. Let's have a look at some of the benefits of being a card-holder.

Good Reasons to Have a Credit Card

Credit cards are great—if they're used responsibly. Many people use credit cards all the time and never run into any trouble with them—or because of them. In fact, a lot of people can't imagine what they'd do without their credit cards.

Credit cards eliminate the need to carry around cash or a checkbook, which is both a safety consideration and a convenience. Let's face it: It's just not smart in most places to walk around with $200 or $300 in your pocket or wallet. Large quantities of money tend to attract attention from the wrong people, and there's no point in taking chances. If somebody steals your cash, it's gone. If somebody steals a credit card, you notify the card issuer and they track your account, but you're not billed for purchases somebody else might make.

There are instances in which you really need a credit card. If you've ever tried to make a hotel reservation without having a credit card, you know how very difficult, or impossible, it is. The same goes for reserving a plane ticket or renting a car. They're also great for ordering stuff from a catalog or for on-line shopping.

There are other good reasons to have a credit card. Used properly, it helps you to build a favorable credit history, and it's a must-have for emergencies.

Establishing a Credit History

Someday, you're going to want to buy a car, take out a loan for college, or even get a mortgage on a house. When these things happen, the lenders you go to will look at your credit history. Your credit history, which you start building as soon as you start charging stuff, will affect your life. It will either help you when you want to borrow money for something

185

important, or it will hurt you. That's why it's really important to establish good credit as soon as you start using it.

A person's credit history is documented in a report that's maintained by a credit agency. There are three big credit agencies in the United States, all of which probably have the same information regarding any given person:

✧ Equifax Credit Services

✧ Trans Union Credit Information Services

✧ Experian

When you apply for your first credit card, your name and all the information you included on the application gets zapped into a computer, and your credit history begins. The agencies that maintain your credit history get information about you from banks, finance companies, credit card suppliers, department stores, and mail order or online companies—anyplace that you do business with. Your credit report also contains personal information such as your social security number, your address, your birth date, job information, and so forth.

Money Matters

Chances are you don't yet have a credit report. If you think you do, you can check with a credit agency and get a copy of it if it exists. Find Equifax at www.equifax.com; Trans Union at www.transunion.com; and Experian at www.experian.com.

When you go to borrow money from a bank or apply for a mortgage, the loan or mortgage person can pull up your credit report and check out whether it makes sense to give you money. If your credit report shows that you pay your bills on time and have little or no outstanding debt, you stand a much better chance of getting a loan or a mortgage than if you're six months behind on your bills and $10,000 in debt.

It used to be that you couldn't get a major credit card without having some kind of credit history—or a parent or other adult to co-sign for the card. You'd have to establish credit with a local department store or have taken out and repaid a loan before you could get a major card. Nowadays you often don't need to have a good credit history—or any credit history—to get a major credit card. Credit card companies are more than happy to hand out cards to practically anybody who wants them, and they'll throw in a T-shirt or a phone calling card in the bargain.

Money Matters

The smartest way to use a credit card is to pay it off every month. In almost all cases, if you're not going to be able to pay for it when the bill comes due, you shouldn't be buying it.

It's important to remember, though, that as soon as you get a card, or even apply for one, you've started writing your own credit history. Using a credit card responsibly will go a long way toward giving you a healthy credit rating.

Emergencies

Another great reason to have a credit card is for emergencies. Your car breaks down and you've got to have it fixed. You go to the next state to visit the kid you met at the beach last summer, only to find out he's moved. It's night, you have no place to stay, and you've got to get a motel room. Your bike disintegrates before your eyes, and it's your only transportation to work. You can't lose the job, so your only choice is to get another bike. In cases such as these, a credit card with your name on it is a very, very welcome sight.

It's tempting sometimes to classify something as an emergency to justify a purchase, but it's important to understand the difference. The burning desire you have for that awesome necklace you saw at the mall does not qualify as an emergency. Neither does the "need" you have for a new pair of black shoes, or the movie you and your girlfriend are just dying to see. Emergencies—real emergencies—are the best reason of all to have a credit card.

Good Reasons Not to Have a Credit Card

Credit cards can be lifesavers, but they've got some big disadvantages, too. If you don't pay them off every month, you're looking at some outrageous interest rates. Even if you do pay them off, there still might be other fees involved. Let's have a look at some costs associated with credit cards.

Talk About High Interest!

Think about this. When you put your hard-earned money in a savings account, the bank gives you about 2 percent interest on it. Yeah, I know—real generous, isn't it? But, when you carry a balance on a credit card, the bank sees fit to charge you 16, 17, even 18 percent interest. Does that seem fair to you? I don't think so!

The interest on credit card debt is about the highest of any interest rate, and it can really add up quickly. If you owe $1,000 on a credit card and you make only the minimum payment each month, you'll be eligible for senior citizen discounts before you get it paid off because of the interest that keeps on accumulating. If you're sitting there right now thinking about the balance on your credit card and it's getting you crazy, consider talking to somebody about it. Credit card debt doesn't go away by itself, you know. If you have a serious problem, you might have to get advice from a financial expert. However, try talking to a parent or other adult that you know first.

Scary Stuff

You can shop around at 15 stores to make sure you're getting the best price on a particular item. However, if you carry a balance on your credit card and are charged a high interest rate, you could easily end up paying two or three times what the item cost.

Annual Fees

If you're paying an annual fee on your credit card, you shouldn't be. There's so much competition among credit card issuers these days that many are willing to waive the annual fee if you ask them to.

If you're paying an annual fee, call the company (there should be a phone number on your monthly statement), and ask to have it waived. If they give you a hard time, tell them you'd like to cancel the card. If they still refuse to waive the fee, find yourself another card company.

Other Fees

Have you ever noticed that banks and companies that issue credit cards seem to like fine print? Check out your policy sometime, or look closely at your monthly statement. Somewhere in all that fine print, you might be surprised to read about other fees that you're not aware of.

Money Matters

It can be really boring, but when you first get a credit card, be sure to read all the information that comes with it very carefully. Then, put it someplace where you'll be able to find it when you need it.

Remember that there's a lot of competition out there when it comes to credit cards, and card issuers are anxious to get your business. If weird fees start showing up on your monthly statement, get on the phone and find out why. If you're not satisfied with the answers, look for another card.

Looking in the Face of Temptation

More dangerous for most people than any fees, however, is the temptation that credit cards can present. Feel like going out for Mexican but have no money? The restaurant takes plastic. You know those boots that are just too awesome and cost $125? You can use the credit card and pay for them later.

These days, just about every place takes credit cards. You can rent the latest movies; eat whatever you want; drink cappuccinos in every flavor; buy all the clothes, CDs, jewelry, and so forth that your heart desires; fill up your gas tank; and even contribute to your favorite charity—all without paying one penny. The only problem is all that spending catches up with you—with interest—at the end of the billing period.

What to Do If Somebody Offers You a Card

Credit cards are easy to get, that's for sure, and high school and college students are prime targets for banks and other card issuers. You know why you're such a hot commodity to credit card companies? The bank or company that gives you the credit card is hoping you're gonna screw up with it and end up owing them big bucks. They're counting on your financial inexperience.

Money Matters

A good rule of thumb is never use a credit card to buy something you won't have anymore when the bill comes around. That means eating out, groceries, gas, renting movies, and so forth.

The National Credit Research Foundation reports that college students owe almost half of the nation's collective $285 billion credit card debt. That's an astounding amount of money for young people to be in debt with. It's such a serious problem that some state legislators are considering putting restrictions on companies that target under-21s for credit cards.

If you want a credit card, you can probably get one. Credit card companies solicit by mail and hang out on college campuses and other places that young people frequent. They're even happy to throw in a free t-shirt, telephone calling card, or restaurant coupons when you fill out and sign one of their applications.

If you're offered a credit card, or five or ten credit cards, think carefully before you sign on the dotted line. If you're offered a card and you want it, be sure you read the entire application carefully before you sign it. Pay especially close attention to these points:

✧ The interest rate and the amount of time for which the rate is guaranteed. Some companies give you a great rate for six months, after which time it doubles or triples.

✧ The annual fee, if any.

✧ The credit limit. (Don't take a higher spending limit than you need—it's too tempting to use it.)

✧ The grace period. This is the amount of time you have to pay off purchases before you start getting charged interest. It used to be 30 days, but is getting shorter and shorter.

✧ Any additional costs, such as discretionary or late fees.

✧ Miscellaneous information that might affect you.

Imagine That

Credit card companies send out nearly 2.5 billion offers for cards every year. That's 10 offers for every man, woman, and child in America. Hard to believe, isn't it!

If you apply for a card just to get the free stuff, make sure you cut it up and throw it away as soon as it comes to you in the mail. Resist the temptation to "test it out"—even once. If you're offered a card that you don't want, don't let a company representative talk you into it. They can be pretty persuasive, so remember that you have an absolute right to say no.

Getting a Card If You Need One

If you want to get a credit card but don't know how to go about it or you're having trouble getting approved for one, there are several things you can do. If you haven't yet applied for a card, you can get an application at your bank or access a bank online that offers credit cards, such as Chase or Citibank. If you're 18 or older and have a job, you'll probably have no trouble getting a card, but you might get a fairly low spending limit ($500 to $1,000) to start. If you keep up with your payments, though, you probably can get that credit limit increased within a year.

If you're not 18, you're 18 but have no credit history and no job, or you've already managed to establish a bad credit history, you might need to get a parent or other adult to co-sign your card. This kind of card is called a secured card, and the adult who signs it is the guarantor. In effect, the adult is guaranteeing the credit card company will get its money, because if you don't pay it, your co-signer becomes responsible for it.

Scary Stuff

Be careful of credit card companies that guarantee unsecured cards to anyone who applies for them, regardless of age, credit history, or work history. They're all over the Internet, and they're—to say the least—suspect.

You'll need to work out with your folks in advance how you'll handle payments, and you should know that most banks require a deposit on a secured card. You or your parents probably will have to hand over an amount equal to the amount of credit you have on the card. If you have a $500 spending limit, your deposit will be $500. Secured cards aren't ideal, but if you need a credit card and can't get an unsecured one, at least it's a start.

Consider carefully whether or not you need a credit card at this point. If you get one, decide from the beginning to use it

193

responsibly. Having a credit card can be a real positive, but it can turn out to be a bummer if you don't use the card wisely. One of the last things you want to do at this point of your life is to wreck your credit rating and set yourself up for huge hassles later on.

The Least You Need to Know

✧ Credit cards have been around since the 1960s, but are used more and more every year.

✧ Credit cards can be great to have and use, but can cause serious problems if you use them to incur more debt than you can pay off.

✧ The bank or company that issues the credit card pays the store for your purchase, and charges you high interest if you don't pay off your credit card bill every month.

✧ Using a credit card responsibly can help you to establish a favorable credit rating, and it's great to have a card handy for emergencies.

✧ Watch out for hidden fees and charges in addition to the regular ones.

✧ Credit cards are plentiful and you probably can get one without too much trouble if you want to.

Chapter 16

The Wonderful World of Investments

In This Chapter

✧ The power of investing early

✧ Letting your money grow, and grow, and grow

✧ Understanding different types of investments

✧ Beginning to understand the stock market

✧ Recognizing the risks to investing

If terms such as bull market, the Dow Jones Industrial Average, tax-deferred savings, mutual funds, and blue chip stock are enough to make you run screaming into your room, just chill for a minute. The stock market is hot, and people of all ages are learning that investing in it can be really fascinating, as well as being the best way to really grow your money. Of course, this doesn't mean you should get online and invest that $100 Aunt Suzy gave you for Christmas. Investing does involve some risks, so you have to know what you're doing before you jump in.

This chapter introduces you to the stock market and other investment vehicles. Mutual funds, money markets, certificates of deposit (CDs), and individual retirement accounts are sound investments for those just starting out. I'll also give you places to go for more information about investing. There's a lot to know, and plenty of places to look if you're interested in learning.

Investing: Not for Adults Only

If you still think of investing money as an adults-only activity, you couldn't be more wrong. Teens and 20-somethings are jumping into the stock market in record numbers, sometimes showing up the old-timers with their earnings. More and more of you also are using investment vehicles such as CDs and money market accounts.

Young people are far more savvy about money and money-related issues than they used to be, and the Internet has made investing a lot easier. You can research, buy, and track stock online without having to pay the fees of a full-service broker. You can obtain information and buy mutual funds, get the latest rates on certificates of deposit, and explore many other investment-related areas.

Scary Stuff

Day trading—which is closely following the stock market and buying and selling stock, often with the intent of hitting it big and making a lot of money—is dangerous business. The average person doesn't know enough about the market to be effective in day trading, and many people have lost a lot of money doing so.

There are plenty of opportunities for investors, both young and not-so-young, but not everyone is ready to start investing in the stock market or buying CDs or mutual funds. Read on to get an idea of whether you should jump in.

Knowing When You're Ready to Start

Financial experts have varying opinions regarding all kinds of money-related topics. However, one thing that nearly everyone agrees on is that the best time to start investing money is when you're young. The more time your money has to grow, the better off you are. It's a simple concept. It's way better to start earning on your money when you're 18 or 20 than it is to wait until you're 35 or 40.

Check out the Motley Fool Web site, located at www.fool.com, for some examples of how starting to save early pays off big time.

Imagine That

The Motley Fools are really brothers David and Tom Gardner, who offer advice on all kinds of finance–related topics in a humorous, friendly way. Their Web site (www. fool.com) includes a special section called Young Fool, which is geared toward teens and those of college age.

The best time to start investing is as early as possible. That doesn't mean that you should jump online or rush out to a brokerage firm to start buying stock. First, you've got to know what you're doing. When you're just starting out in investing, it's a really good idea to find somebody to help you. This could be a broker, who is a person trained to buy and sell investments; or an adult you know who has knowledge of the stock market or other investment vehicles.

Money Matters

The Internet is a great place, but remember that there's a lot of information out there that's just not right. Whether placed there intentionally or not, there's lots of erroneous stuff. Don't ever rely on stock tips you see on the Net.

Another idea might be to join an investment club, which is a group of people who pool their money to buy stocks or other investments. Belonging to an investment club is a great learning experience, because each member is required to re-search companies and learn about buying and selling stock.

Investment clubs have been around for a long time, but they're more popular today than ever before. Most clubs don't require huge contributions, and members like them be-cause they learn a lot about the stock market and investing.

It doesn't make any sense to take steps toward investing, though, if you don't have any money or if you owe money. Understand that you don't need a lot of money to begin in-vesting; but obviously, you do need some.

Money Matters

To learn a whole lot more about investment clubs, grab a copy of *The Complete Idiot's Guide to Starting an Investment Club,* by Sarah Young Fisher and Susan Shelly.

If you owe money on a credit card, don't even think about investing. The best investment you can make is to pay off that high-interest money eater. It makes no sense to invest money to earn 12 or 13 percent when the interest rate on your credit card debt is 18 or 20 percent. However, if you're debt free and have some money saved up, you might seriously want to think about investing.

Different Kinds of Investments

To most people, thoughts of investing money conjure up images of the stock market; and for those who take the time to learn about stocks and understand the risks involved with buying them, the stock market might be a good place to invest. However, there are different kinds of investments from the stock market, some of which might make more sense for a beginning investor.

Even the savings account that you might already have is a type of investment, although at 2 or 3 percent interest, it is not a very good one. Some better investments for people just testing out the financial waters are mutual funds, money market funds, and certificates of deposit. If you happen to have a job with a company that offers a 401(k) plan (an employer-sponsored retirement plan to which you contribute a portion of your income to grow, tax-deferred, until you retire), make sure you take advantage of it.

Employers who offer 401(k) plans often match employees' contributions, which is like getting free money. If Tom has $50 taken out of his paycheck every two weeks and put into his 401(k) savings, and his employer matches his contribution, lucky Tom is doubling his investment.

Money contributed to a 401(k) plan goes into investment options that the employee chooses. Companies often will have financial advisors available to advise employees about the best choices for their investments. Let's take a closer look at some of these investment options.

Imagine That

The 401(k) savings plan was introduced in 1982 as a way for employers to save the money they'd been putting into pension plans for their employees.

A Money Market and CD Review

You learned a little about money market accounts and certificates of deposit in Chapter 9, "Making Your Money Work for You" so you should recall that a money market account is really a kind of savings account that generally pays a little higher interest than a regular account.

There's another type of money market called a money market fund (MMF). This is a specialized *mutual fund* (an investment in which a professional portfolio manager places the money of many investors in stocks, bonds, and other holdings) that pays you interest on your investment. It's different from a money market account in several ways.

Money market funds are held within mutual fund companies and are not insured, unlike money market accounts, which are insured by FDIC. That of course makes MMFs riskier than money market accounts; but as you might have guessed, the earning potential is greater in a fund than in an account. And even though MMFs are not insured, most mutual fund companies try to keep them safe enough so that the risk you take is very small. They are considered to be safe short-term investments, and some offer tax advantages.

Certificates of Deposit

Certificates of deposit (CDs) are accounts in which you deposit money for a specified amount of time—usually between three months and several years. You usually earn more interest on your money in a CD than you would in a savings or money market account, but you have to let the money sit for the required time or suffer a penalty. A minimum amount of money also is required to open a CD. Some kinds of CDs require $1,000 or more to get started, but others require $500 or even less.

Most CDs pay fixed interest rates, meaning you'll know up front how much interest your money will earn, and the rate won't change during the time your money is invested. Some CDs do offer variable rates, meaning that the interest rates can fluctuate during the time your money is invested.

If you're interested in opening a CD, be sure to shop around—you don't have to open it where you have a savings or checking account.

Mutual Funds

Mutual funds are the most popular form of investment for individuals; there are several reasons for this. The biggest reason probably is that you don't need much money to get into a mutual fund. Some will let you in for as little as $50. This makes them very appealing, especially to younger investors.

Mutual funds pool the money of many investors to buy stocks, bonds, and other investments. Professional portfolio managers (also called fund managers) and researchers decide what to buy. When you invest money in a mutual fund, you're really investing in whatever the portfolio manager decides to buy. You might own stocks or bonds in companies that you've never even heard of.

Think of a mutual fund as a big pie. When you hand over some of your money to buy into a mutual fund, you get back a slice of pie. If the value of the mutual fund increases, the pie—and your slice of it—gets bigger. If the value decreases, the pie—and your slice—gets smaller.

The diversity of mutual funds is appealing to many people. Diversity in this sense means that the money you invest is spread around over a wide range of stocks and bonds. This makes it very unlikely that the fund will ever lose its entire value. One aspect of the fund might decrease in value; another increases. Mutual funds carry almost no risk of going bankrupt.

Money Matters

If you're interested in learning more about mutual funds— a lot more—check out *The Complete Idiot's Guide to Making Money in Mutual Funds,* by Alan Lavine and Gail Liberman.

The following list contains some facts about different types of mutual funds.

✧ There are mutual funds that you can purchase directly from the mutual fund company, without having to pay a broker to do it for you.

✧ Mutual funds that let you avoid paying a sales commission on your transaction are called no-load funds. The mutual fund companies provide 800 numbers that you can call for recommendations on what funds to buy.

✧ Funds that charge a sales commission are called load funds. If you invest $100 in a load mutual fund, $5 (or whatever the percentage rate is) is taken out of your investment to pay the salesperson.

✧ There are different kinds of mutual funds, some of which involve more risk than others. Some invest heavily in stocks (stock funds), others in bonds (bond funds), and still others (hybrid funds) are spread around over both.

✧ Balanced funds hold about equal parts of stocks and bonds, and present a lower risk than some other types of mutual funds.

✧ Global and international funds invest money in companies located in various parts of the world, either in addition to U.S. companies or excluding U.S. companies. Some mutual funds, called emerging market funds, invest in companies located in countries where the markets aren't yet developed, but are thought by analysts to be about to do so.

✧ Sector funds invest in only one kind of investment, such as technology or health care.

If you're looking to start investing some money, mutual funds might be a good option. However, as with any investment, make sure you understand what you're doing and the risks involved before jumping in.

Individual Retirement Accounts

Anyone who makes any money by working can contribute up to $2,000 per year in an individual retirement account (IRA). Money you put into an IRA is tax-deferred and probably tax-deductible. That means you don't have to pay any taxes on it until you take it out of the fund when you retire, and you get to deduct the amount you contribute from your taxable income.

If you earn money and don't report it, you're out of luck as far as an IRA goes. You can't contribute to an IRA if you earn—but don't pay—taxes. Sorry about that. So, even if you earn $3,000 a year from your lawn care/snow removal business, you can't get into an IRA if you don't report the income. You could, however, be risking trouble if the Internal Revenue Service ever comes knocking at your door.

The idea behind IRAs is that you'll invest your money and leave it in the fund to earn interest until you retire. You can get your money before retirement if you need it, but you'll pay a pretty hefty penalty.

Money Matters

You'll pay no tax on a tax-deferred investment until you take your money out of it. A tax-deductible investment is one that reduces the amount of your taxable income.

A variation of the basic IRA is the Roth IRA. Basically, a Roth IRA is different from a regular one in the way that your contributions are taxed. When you contribute to a regular IRA, your money isn't taxed until you take it out of the fund. With a Roth IRA, your money is taxed before you contribute to the fund. So what's the advantage, you ask? Your money accumulates in the fund (including the interest) tax free. If you leave your money in a Roth IRA for at least five years, you can get it, and the interest you've earned, without paying any more taxes on it.

There's also an IRA called an educational IRA, which is set up especially to fund education expenses. And there's an SEP-IRA, which is a retirement plan for people who are self-employed.

It probably seems to you that you're too young to start thinking about saving for retirement. After all, you want to save for a car, and college, and the post-prom trip to the beach, and all those other things. But, retirement? Just remember that the best time to start saving and investing for anything is when you're young, with lot of time to let your money grow.

A Beginner's Guide to the Stock Market

Now that you have a basic understanding of some other investment options, let's take a look at stock and the stock market. What is the stock market, exactly, and how does it work? How do investors make—or lose—money in the stock market?

Money Matters

To learn more about the stock market, see *The Complete Idiot's Guide to Making Money on Wall Street*, by Christy Heady.

The stock market is a generic term that we use to describe the organized arena in which securities are traded. Securities are simply investments—either stocks or bonds. The three biggest stock exchanges in the United States are as follows:

✧ **The New York Stock Exchange.** The largest organized stock exchange in the country, the New York Stock Exchange was formed in 1792.

✧ **The American Stock Exchange.** With less stringent listing requirements than the New York Stock Exchange, the American Stock Exchange attracts and lists many smaller companies. It was known before 1951 as the American Curb Exchange because trading was conducted on the curb of Wall and Broad streets in New York City.

✧ **The National Association of Securities Dealers Automated Quotation System.** The NASDAQ, unlike the other two major exchanges, has no physical location. Trading is all done by computer.

You'll often hear on the radio or TV, or hear people say that the stock market is up, or the market is down. The overall performance of the stock market is measured in many ways. One measure—the one you can hear each day—is the Dow Jones Industrial Average (DJIA).

Imagine That

When the market moves upward over a period of time, it's called a bull market. When it moves downward, it's called a bear market.

The DJIA is a group of 30 stocks with a daily average. It goes up or down, depending on the average price of those 30 stocks. If the average value of those stocks has increased, we say the DJIA has gone up. If the value of the stocks decrease, we say the DJIA is down. There are other measures of the stock market as well, but the DJIA is most commonly used.

When you trade in the stock market, what you're doing is buying and selling securities. Let's have a look at how stocks and bonds are different, and how investors (hopefully) make money from them.

Stock is something you buy and own. You buy stock because you hope it will increase in value, and you'll be able to sell it and make a profit. When you buy stock in a company, you're really buying a little piece of that company. A company sells those little pieces of itself to raise money. Stock is sold in units called shares and, when you buy some, you become a shareholder in the company.

The ideal is to be able to buy stock when it's cheap, hold onto it until it increases in value, and then sell it. As you can imagine, that scenario doesn't always play out. The value of stock can fall, meaning that the shareholder has lost money.

There are a lot of different kinds of stock, some of which carry a lot more risk than others. Some of these stocks and their definitions are listed in the glossary at the back of this book.

Bonds are another type of investment. With bonds, you don't own—you loan. When you buy a bond, you're lending your money to an organization such as the U.S. government or a corporation. The organization uses your money, and in exchange agrees to pay you interest on your money, and to return it to you after an agreed-upon period of time.

Just as there are different kinds of stock, there are different kinds of bonds; and as with stock, some involve more risk than others. You read about some of the different types of bonds in Chapter 9.

No investment, whether it's stock, bonds, real estate, or whatever, is without some risk. It's possible that you'll buy stock or bonds, just before the entire market undergoes a drastic downturn. It's possible that you'll buy land, only to have the entire area be devalued because it's discovered to be polluted.

The key to making any investment is to research carefully and fully understand what you're doing. Starting to invest your money at an early age is really great, and if you do it properly, you'll be really glad that you did when you get older. If you invest your money in junk, however, you'll have wasted a lot of time and money; but at least you'll have time to get back on track.

The Least You Need to Know

✧ There are many ways to invest your money, some of which make more sense for teenagers than others.

✧ The earlier you begin investing, the more time your money has to grow and work for you.

✧ Money markets and certificates of deposit are safe, although not very exciting investments.

✧ Mutual funds are extremely popular, mostly because you don't need much money to begin investing in them.

✧ Individual retirement accounts offer tax advantages on the money that you save for when you retire.

✧ The stock market offers good opportunity to make money—if you know what you're doing.

Chapter 17

Myself, Inc.
Founder- Me.
CEO- Me.

Thinking About a Business of Your Own

In This Chapter

✧ Meeting teens who have already started businesses

✧ Looking at what teen entrepreneurs are doing

✧ Understanding what it takes to be an entrepreneur

✧ Considering the good, the bad, and the ugly

✧ Planning now for your own business

One of the definitions of an *entrepreneur* in *Webster's New 20th Century Unabridged Dictionary* is "a person who organizes and directs a business undertaking, assuming the risk for the sake of the profit." Although that definition is adequate, I don't think it's complete. An entrepreneur is far more than that. An entrepreneur is an adventurer—a risk taker. An entrepreneur is someone who looks past the status quo, who wonders why things can't be done better. An entrepreneur is brave, enthusiastic, motivated, determined, and persistent. A real entrepreneur is a person who sets a goal, wants it badly, and refuses to give up on his or her way to attain it.

We admire entrepreneurs in this country. We look up to people who start and grow their own businesses, who are their own bosses, and who make their own rules. Many teenagers are jumping into the entrepreneurial arena and they're starting to be noticed and looked up to, as well. In this chapter, we'll look at who some of these teenage entrepreneurs are and what they're doing. We'll discuss some of the benefits and risks of starting your own business—the advantages and disadvantages. You'll also have a chance to evaluate yourself to see if you might have what it takes to be an entrepreneur.

Teenage Entrepreneurs

There have always been teenage entrepreneurs. The kids you see pushing lawn mowers up and down the streets in the summertime, looking for a yard that needs to be mowed; the ones that grow flowers in a backyard garden and go door to door selling bouquets of them; the teens that shovel snow, start baby-sitting and dog-walking businesses, or organize cleaning services—all of them are entrepreneurs.

Money Matters

We often think of entrepreneurs as people like Donald Trump or Bill Gates, but there also are hundreds of entrepreneurs in your own community of all ages, races, and income levels.

Entrepreneurial spirit abounds, even in little kids. Pay attention in the summertime to kids who set up lemonade stands or sell apples they pick from the trees in their backyards. Even little kids can weed a garden for a neighbor or gather newspapers for somebody who's away.

The truth is that the desire to be an entrepreneur comes naturally to a lot of people. The hard part is turning that desire into an enterprise that works. It's not as easy as feeling that you'd like to do something; however, that's not to say that it can't be done.

Who Are They?

Who are these teenage entrepreneurs who are making the news—not to mention the money? Let's have a look at some examples:

Mike Nowotarski, an 18-year-old from St. Petersburg, Florida, turned his entrepreneurial inclinations into a successful video production business. He began working with video production as a high school sophomore and loved it. He stayed heavily involved in his school's TV crew, and by the time he was nearing graduation, he felt he was good enough to get paid for production work.

Nowotarski's dad lent him money for the basic equipment he'd need and set him up with their family's lawyer to oversee the legal work necessary for starting a company. He opened his company, Premier Productions, in November 1999. Ten months later he'd earned $10,000. He's currently in college, studying video while continuing to run his company.

Money Matters

To get an overview of what 100 young entrepreneurs have done, go to www.youngbiz.com and check out the YoungBiz 100.

Nowotarski's friends, Craig Brandys and Justin Griego, also have started their own company, through which they design Web sites. They expected to make $30,000 during their first full year in business.

In an article published in the *St. Petersburg Times*, Brandys said the idea to start his own business came to him one morning as he was lying in bed, trying to find the energy to crawl out and go back to his job at a local steak house. Brandys was a host there, working eight-hour shifts that sometimes turned into double shifts, and earning $6 an hour. "I was sick of it," Brandys was quoted as saying. "One morning I was in bed and really couldn't motivate myself to get up and go to work. I called Justin up and said, 'Hey, let's found a company to design Web sites and make a lot of money.'" And that's what they did.

Leigh Taylor, a 17-year-old from Dewey, Oklahoma, earns $400 per month training horses for other people. She started her business when someone who had observed her with her own horses asked her to train a horse for his daughter. Taylor says she spends between 10 and 12 hours a week on her business.

Imagine That

Young entrepreneurs are calling themselves "treps," an abbreviated take on a word that's hard to say, and even harder to spell. Young entrepreneurs who operate on the net are eTreps.

Alejandra Torres is only 13, but she's earning $120 as a child-care provider and investing most of the money she earns in mutual funds. She lives on a military base in Oahu, Hawaii, where there are a lot of kids, and she often watches as many as five at a time. She charges $2 an hour per child.

Anand Shimpi, the 18-year-old from Raleigh, North Carolina who was *YoungBiz* magazine's top entrepreneur of 1999, reports almost $1 million in yearly revenues.

Brad Ogden, 18, of Detroit, who ranks in the first five of *YoungBiz's* top 100 entrepreneurs, owns and operates Virtual Webpages, a Web design company that earned more than half a million dollars in 1999.

These are just a few examples of teenagers who have launched successful businesses. No doubt, there are thousands of you out there. Not all of these young entrepreneurs are making a million, or half a million, or even more than a couple of thousand dollars a year; but they are making money. Statistics that *YoungBiz* magazine gathered show that at least 60 percent of teenage entrepreneurs earn more than they would if they worked at The Gap or the local steak house. The average income of those on *YoungBiz's* top 100 list for 1999 was $28,000.

What Are They Doing?

Although the young entrepreneurs who are making the most money tend to be in computer-related endeavors, there are teens out there with companies whose products range from earthworms to handmade art-deco benches. The following are some of the great businesses listed in *YoungBiz* magazine's 1999 list of the top 100 entrepreneurs:

✧ Tim Thorpe, 16, of LaFayette, New York made about $8,000 in two months selling pumpkins to use for jack-o-lanterns and pies.

✧ Chase Harps, 15, of Atlanta, Georgia, earns between $150 and $200 per week selling cologne that he produces.

✧ Christina Smith, 15, of Brooklyn, New York, earns about $75 per week selling personalized accessories, such as leashes and collars, for small dogs. She decorates them with ethnic, Aztec, and flower patterns.

✧ Maggie and Allie Cawood-Smith, both age 12, of Auburn, California make between $50 and $100 per week selling the lip balm they make out of natural ingredients. The twins sell to stores and individuals.

✧ Brad Sweet, 18, of Relay, Maryland sells an average of 20 custom birdhouses per year for $75 to $300 each.

✧ Jeff Wahl, 16, of Binghamton, New York earns about $235 per week teaching dance lessons to adults and youth. He also choreographs shows for local music programs.

As you can see, there's great diversity in what these young entrepreneurs are doing.

Knowing If You Have What It Takes

People start businesses for all kinds of reasons. Some do so because they want to make millions of dollars and retire when they're 50. Others want to create products and services that will help others and improve society. Some want to provide a good life for their families; others just can't stand the thought of having a boss and having to show up at a job every day for the next 40 years.

Psychologists who have studied entrepreneurs say that the primary reason that people start and successfully run their own businesses is because they feel the need to achieve something. A recent article in the *Harvard Business Review* says that drive for achievement, or the desire to do something better or more efficiently than it's been done before, is the strongest motivator for entrepreneurs. Some other common motivators include: a desire for power and/or wealth, a need to fulfill an inner drive or to succeed, a desire to escape from a traditional work situation or to be one's own boss, and a desire to fulfill a dream.

Some personal qualities that are common to most entrepreneurs include the following:

- ✧ Well-organized
- ✧ A self-starter
- ✧ Innovative
- ✧ Flexible and adaptable
- ✧ Able to solve problems
- ✧ Able to deal with and overcome obstacles
- ✧ Able to make decisions
- ✧ A good communicator
- ✧ Energetic
- ✧ Optimistic
- ✧ Determined
- ✧ Responsible
- ✧ Confident
- ✧ Persistent

Scary Stuff

If your work ethic—that thing inside that motivates you to do your work well and take pride in it—doesn't work so well, you'll need to improve it before jumping into starting a business. If you don't, you'll be setting yourself up to fail.

Having been on this earth for however many years you have, you probably have a pretty good idea of your strengths and weaknesses by now. To figure out whether you've got the

right stuff to be an entrepreneur, look at the personal qualities and sources of motivations in the preceding list. Then,
being very, very honest with yourself, ask if those motivations and personal qualities apply to you.

If you think about starting your own business, you'd better
be as honest with yourself as you can when deciding whether
you have what it takes. If you're not, you'll be sure to find
out—and maybe be very surprised—once you get started.

The Highs and Lows of Entrepreneurship

Owning and running your own business sounds great, and it
can be. In the course of doing business you'll no doubt meet
up with all kinds of interesting people. You'll get to know
about suppliers and how a business runs, the ins and outs of
daily operations, how to write and execute a business plan,
and more. You'll probably become acquainted with members
of the community in which you live, and you'll become
known as your business grows.

Starting your own business might sound great; and hopefully,
it will be great. You'll have no boss (other than yourself), no
time clock to worry about, and all the holidays and weekends
off that you care to take. If you think, though, that being an
entrepreneur is all fame, fun, and glory, take a minute right
now for a reality check. Entrepreneurs will tell you that it's
not quite like that. Entrepreneurs who have started small
businesses—from the ground up—will tell you that it's more
like long, long hours; an uncertain (at best) salary; really hard
work; more long hours; and a lot of headaches. Sure, there
are good times, and a lot of advantages; still, starting and
running your own business isn't easy.

For the reasons previously listed, and other reasons, more
than half of all start-up businesses fail. That's something that
anyone thinking about opening a business should know. The
chef who finally opens his own restaurant never stops to
consider that he'll be in the restaurant all day Saturday, every
Saturday night, then back again in time to prepare dinner
for Sunday, while his family participates in weekend events

without him. The teen who starts her own dog walking business neglects to think about the fact that dogs need to be walked every morning, even when she doesn't have to get up for school and would rather sleep in.

Money Matters

If you try to start a business and the business fails, it doesn't make you a failure. All it means is that you have to re-evaluate and do things smarter the next time around. Failing is never trying to do something you really want to do.

These statistics and stories aren't meant to scare or discourage you, but it's important to understand what owning your own business entails. If you can, find somebody who's already done it and talk to him or her about what is involved. No doubt topics such as taxes, filling orders on time, paperwork, juggling schedules to balance personal and work lives, and hiring and training employees will be mentioned. Hopefully, topics such as a great feeling of satisfaction, good financial rewards, a sense of belonging in the community, and a lot of personal satisfaction also will apply.

Planning Now for What You'll Do Later

So, you think you want to start your own business, do you? Good for you. If that's the case, it's not too early to start planning, even if you won't really be getting the business underway for several years.

There are a lot of things to consider: What kind of business makes the most sense for you to start, and in what area can you be most successful? Should you go it alone, or plan to work with a partner? Where will your business be based? Do you have the necessary equipment, or will you have to buy it? What legal structure will your business have? How will you pay for start-up costs? All of these questions must be addressed and thought through. A business plan, which serves as a kind of road map, can help you to do that.

Every business, no matter how small or how big, needs to have a business plan. It forces you to clearly state what you want to do, and how you plan to do it; and it lets others know what you're doing, as well.

Money Matters

To get an outline of the Small Business Association's business plan, go to http://www.sbaonline.sba.gov/starting/businessplan.html. It's right there for you to use.

To see an outline of a business plan and to access a lot of other good information about starting and running a company, check out the Small Business Association Web site at www.sba.gov. The Small Business Association is a government agency that assists entrepreneurs by providing management and technical assistance. It will give you information about taxes, marketing, and so forth.

A good business plan will serve as a guide for how your company will start and grow. It also will be an important marketing tool.

A business plan not only gives you an idea of what you should be doing at a particular time; it lets everyone else know what you're doing. A good business plan can get people interested in what you're doing. It might even inspire them to assist you, either financially or in another way. The main part of your business plan should include a description of your business, your marketing plan (how you'll promote your business), your financial plan (how you'll get the money to start and run your business), and your management plan (how you'll run your business).

Other parts of the plan include a cover sheet, a summary, a statement of purpose, a table of contents, and any supporting material you might have.

If all this sounds worse than studying for the hardest final you've ever had, try not to be discouraged. A business plan is nothing more than a statement of what you plan to do and how you plan to do it. It doesn't have to be complicated, or 50 pages long, or written in fancy legal language. It just needs to be a clear picture of what you plan to accomplish.

Money Matters

For more information about and help with business plans, see *Your First Business Plan: A Simple Question and Answer Format Designed to Help You Write Your Own Plan,* by Joseph Covello and Brian J. Hazelgren.

If you're serious about starting a business, get a plan in place and then talk to adults who might be in a position to help you. You'll need to learn about laws in your area that pertain to small businesses, and other matters that might require advice. Check with your local Chamber of Commerce to see if it provides free services to entrepreneurs who are thinking of starting a business. In some communities, retired business people serve as resources and are happy to share their knowledge and expertise.

Having your own business can be exciting, challenging, fun, and profitable. If you truly want to start a business, and your personality is such that you believe you can make it work, go ahead. Believe that you'll succeed. Believe that you'll learn a lot, have fun, and ultimately, make a lot of money. Just don't forget that starting a business also brings a lot of work and responsibility, too.

The Least You Need to Know

✧ Teenage entrepreneurs are on the increase, and they're gaining the attention and admiration of many.

✧ Teen-run e-businesses abound, but they're not the only games in town.

✧ Being an entrepreneur requires certain characteristics, so think hard about whether or not you're suited to the job.

✧ Owning and running a business requires lots of hard work and there's no guarantee that you'll make money, but it also can be rewarding and fun.

✧ Every business needs a business plan, and it's never too early to get started.

Glossary

allowance philosophy   Schools of thought concerning allowance, such as whether it should be given and on what merit it should be given.

American Stock Exchange   One of the major exchanges of the U.S. stock market.

annual fee   A fee you pay each year for the privilege of having the use of a credit card or other membership.

assets   Everything on the positive side of your balance sheet such as savings, property, stocks, cars, IRAs, and so forth.

automated teller machine   A machine introduced in about 1980 at which individuals can conduct banking transactions such as transferring funds or accessing cash from their accounts.

balanced funds   Mutual funds that hold about equal parts stocks and bonds and present a lower risk than some other types of mutual funds.

bankrupt   The condition of having been legally declared insolvent, or having no money to meet liabilities.

bankruptcy   The legal act or process of applying for relief from debts under the bankruptcy law.

bartering   is simply the exchange of goods or services between two people or groups of people. Historians agree that bartering is the oldest form of exchange and probably was used practically from the beginning of humankind.

bond   A debt instrument. The issuer promises to pay the investor a specified amount of interest for a period of time and to repay the principal at maturity.

bond fund   A mutual fund that invests heavily in bonds.

broker   A person who earns a commission or fee for acting as an agent in making contracts or sales.

budget   A schedule of income and expenses commonly broken into monthly intervals and typically covering a one-year period.

business plan   A detailed description of your business and your plans for running it. A business plan is intended to serve as a guide, and also serves as a marketing tool.

certificate of deposit (CD)   A receipt for a deposit of funds in a financial institution that permits the holder to receive interest, plus the deposit, after a specified amount of time.

commercial bank   A financial institution, chartered by either the federal or state government, that takes deposits, loans money, and provides other services to individuals or corporations.

compound interest   Interest paid on interest from previous periods in addition to principal. Basically, compounding interest involves adding interest to principal and any previous interest to calculate interest in the next period. Compound interest can be figured daily, monthly, quarterly, semi-annually, or annually.

corporate bond   A bond issued by a corporation as opposed to one issued by the government.

cowrie shell   The shell of a snail-like creature that was used as a common form of currency, starting in about 1200 B.C. in China.

credit agency   An agency that processes and stores information concerning the credit histories of individuals. The information is used to assess a person's credit worthiness. The three big credit agencies in the United States are Equifax Credit Services, Trans Union Credit Information Services, and Experian.

credit card   A plastic card used to purchase goods or services with the agreement that, although no money is exchanged at the time, you'll be billed, and will pay for, your purchase.

credit history   A record of an individual's past events that pertain to credit previously given or applied for.

credit union   A nonprofit, cooperative financial institution providing credit to its members who share a common bond such as a place of employment. Credit unions often pay slightly higher rates of interest on savings accounts and charge lower rates on consumer loans.

currency   A medium of trade or exchange.

day trading   The practice of closely following the stock market and buying and selling stock often with the intent of realizing high profits.

debit card   A plastic card used for purchasing goods and services or obtaining cash advances in which payment is made from existing funds in a bank account.

discretionary expenses   An expense that's not necessary such as vacations, memberships, and entertainment.

Dow Jones Industrial Average (DJIA)   One of the measures of the stock market that includes averages for utilities, industrial, and transportation stocks, as well as the composite averages.

educational IRA   An individual retirement account set up especially to fund education expenses.

emerging market funds   Mutual funds that invest in companies located in countries where the markets aren't yet developed, but are thought by analysts to be about to do so.

entrepreneur   A person who organizes and directs a business undertaking, assuming the risk for the sake of the profit.

expenses   Any and all charges for goods and services that you use, whether necessary or unnecessary.

Fair Labor Standards Act (FLSA)   There are certain jobs that are prohibited under the FLSA for all youth under the age of 18.

Federal Deposit Insurance Corporation (FDIC)   An independent deposit insurance corporation established by

Congress as part of the Banking Act of 1933. Banks pay the FDIC to insure individual deposits within them, thereby protecting their customers from possible loss.

financing   When you agree to pay for something you buy over a certain amount of time, usually with the understanding that you'll pay interest on the amount of money you owe.

fixed expenses   Expenses that don't vary much in amount from month to month such as rent, car payments, or membership dues.

401(k) plan   An employer-sponsored retirement plan that lets you contribute a portion of your current salary into a tax-deferred fund. You get back the money, plus the interest you earn on it, when you retire, at which time taxes are due.

front-end installment loan   A loan that requires you to pay interest on the entire loan, even after you've paid some of it back.

global fund   A mutual fund that includes at least 25 percent foreign securities. The value of the fund depends on the health of foreign economies and exchange rate movements.

gold standard   A monetary standard that links a nation's money supply to its stock of monetary gold. Under the gold standard, all currency used within a country had to be backed by gold that the country possessed. It was adopted in the U.S. in 1900 and was discontinued in the 1930s.

government bond   A bond issued by the government, as opposed to one issued by a corporation.

grant   Money or other aid given for a specific use, usually as a gift, without the requirement of payback.

high-yield bond   A high-risk, high-yield debt security issued by corporations or municipalities that are considered to be of low quality.

hybrid funds   Mutual funds that are spread fairly evenly around stocks and bonds.

individual retirement account (IRA) A retirement savings plan in which you can contribute up to $2,000 per year. Funds can grow tax-deferred until they are withdrawn at retirement. Contributions may or may not be tax-deductible, depending on how much money you make and if you're participating in any other retirement savings plans.

interest The cost for the use of borrowed money. You receive interest when you allow a bank or other form of investment to use your money. You pay interest when you borrow money from a bank or other source.

interest-bearing account An account that pays you interest for having your money invested there.

international fund A mutual fund that invests only outside the country in which the fund is located.

Internet bank A type of bank that is operated electronically, with all transactions conducted by computer.

investment The process of purchasing securities or property for which stability of value and level of expected returns are somewhat predictable.

investment club A group of people who form a club for the purpose of investing money in mutually agreed-upon securities.

investment personalities Categories assigned to investors based on their attitudes and philosophies concerning factors such as risk tolerance, perspective on change and the future, and control issues.

leasing When you agree to pay a specified amount of money for a specified period of time in exchange for the use of a product such as a car.

liability Anything that falls on the negative side of your net worth, such as a mortgage or debt.

load fund A mutual fund with shares sold at a price that includes a sales charge.

minimum wage   The least amount a worker can be paid by a company or firm. Minimum wage is established by the federal government but can vary from state to state, depending on state law.

modern barter   A method of barter that connects people or groups of people electronically and allows them to trade a variety of goods and services. The practice also is gaining in popularity among companies, which trade commodities ranging from advertising to hotel rooms.

money market account   Accounts held with banks and insured by the FDIC.

money market fund   A mutual fund with a non-fluctuating $1 investment value per share. Held within mutual fund companies, they are not insured but generally are considered to be safe investments.

municipal bond   A bond issued by a city, county, state, or other political entity.

mutual fund   An open-ended investment company that invests its shareholders' money in a diversified group of securities. Mutual funds usually are diverse and professionally managed.

National Association of Securities Dealers Automated Quotation System (NASDAQ)   One of the major exchanges of the U.S. stock market.

net worth   The amount of wealth you own, calculated by taking the total value of assets owned and subtracting all liabilities.

New York Stock Exchange   One of the major exchanges of the U.S. stock market.

no-load fund   A mutual fund sold without a sales charge. No-load funds sell directly to customers at net asset value with no intermediate salesperson charging a fee.

non-discretionary expenses   Necessary expenses such as housing, food, utilities, and taxes.

non-routine expenses   Expenses that don't occur regularly, such as repair bills, medical bills, or wedding gifts.

personal identification number (PIN)   A number assigned to an individual to be used with a debit card or automated teller machine. The number allows the individual to access his or her accounts.

portfolio manager   A person who is paid a fee to supervise the investments of others. A person who manages a mutual fund is called a portfolio manager, or fund manager.

principal   The capital sum, as distinguished from interest or profit.

public transportation   Transportation other than one's own vehicle including buses, trains, and subways. Public transportation is the most efficient way to transport the greatest number of people in a largely populated area.

Roth IRA   An individual retirement account in which the funds placed into the account are non-tax-deductible. If held for more than five years, all funds withdrawn are received tax-free. The Roth IRA was first introduced in 1998.

routine expenses   Expenses that remain relatively the same, week after week or month after month, such as rent, insurance, food, and entertainment.

salary scale   The system by which an employer pays employees. A salary scale includes an explanation of how raises are given, how salaries are established, and so forth.

savings bond   *See* treasury bond.

scholarship   A specific gift of money or other aid to help a student continue in his or her studies.

sector funds   Mutual funds that invest in only one kind of investment such as technology or health care.

securities   Investments that represent evidence of debt, ownership of a business, or the legal right to sell an ownership interest in a business. For general purposes, securities are stocks and bonds.

SEP-IRA   A type of individual retirement account designed for people who are self-employed.

simple interest   Interest paid on an initial investment only. Simple interest is calculated by multiplying the principal times the annual rate of interest times the number of years involved.

simple interest loan   A loan that lets you pay interest only on the money you still owe on your loan, not on the original amount of the loan.

Small Business Association (SBA)   One of the U.S. government agencies that assists entrepreneurs by offering information, funding, and other resources.

spending categories   General areas within which you spend money such as entertainment, clothing, housing, education, or transportation.

social responsibility   A sense of understanding your place in the world, and your responsibility to contribute to the greater good of society.

stock   Shares of ownership in a company.

stock fund   A mutual fund that invests heavily in stock.

stock market   The organized securities exchanges for stock and bond transactions. Major exchanges are the New York Stock Exchange, the American Stock Exchange, and the National Association of Securities Dealers Automated Quotation System (NASDAQ).

tax-deductible   An expense that can be used to offset gross income when calculating your taxable gross income.

tax-deferred   Income that is earned, but is not received or taxed until a later date.

thrift   A financial institution that derives its funds primarily from consumer savings accounts set up to provide personal mortgages. "Thrift" usually refers to savings and loan associations, but other financial institutions also can be thrifts.

treasury bond   A longer-term bond of the U.S. Treasury, available through a bank or brokerage firm, or directly from the Federal Reserve. Commonly called a savings bond.

trust   A legal document that holds money, property, or other assets for the beneficiary to receive at a designated time in the future.

variable expenses   Expenses that change from month to month such as vacations, food, or entertainment.

wampum   Strings of beads made from clam shells that North American Indians, and later colonists, used as money.

will   A legal document that instructs how a person's assets are to be divided at the time of his or her death. It also might contain special instructions about how the assets are to be treated, or information concerning disposal of the person's body, funeral services, and so forth.

Tips and Tricks for Saving Money

25 Tips for Saving Money on Just About Everything

1. Buy cases of soda and take one with you instead of buying singles from the machine. Ditto for juice and water.

2. Pack a lunch instead of buying it. You'll save money and probably eat healthier, too.

3. Don't overlook second-hand stores for clothes, especially expensive items such as coats.

4. Look for stores that sell second-hand sporting and recreational equipment such as rollerblades, bikes, and camping gear.

5. Don't go into a store unless you need something. Browsing can be an expensive hobby.

6. When eating in a restaurant, ask for water and skip the soda.

7. Ask your friends to come to your house and chip in for pizza instead of going out to eat in a restaurant.

8. Remember that fast food isn't cheap, and limit your trips to the drive-through.

9. Don't buy clothes that need to be dry-cleaned.

10. Wear what you own instead of buying new clothes all the time.

11. If you see something in a store that you like, ask a salesperson if the item will be going on sale soon.

12. Swap special-occasion clothes with your friends instead of buying something you'll wear only once.

13. Borrow shoes for a dance instead of buying new ones.

14. Buy items such as tights or underwear in packs of four or six.

15. Do your own nails or get a friend to do them instead of paying for manicures.

16. Get a good haircut from a stylist; then use a cheaper place for in-
between maintenance.

17. Look for store brands or less expensive varieties of items such as shampoo and shower gel.

18. Clip and use coupons for things you buy or activities that you
participate in.

19. Exercise in shorts and a T-shirt instead of spending your money on the latest Nike exercise fashions. They might look good, but they don't improve your workout.

20. Borrow books from the library instead of buying paper-backs that you read once and stick on a shelf.

21. Borrow CDs from friends and listen before you buy them.

22. Take care of the things you have so they won't need to be replaced.

23. Cancel subscriptions to magazines that you don't have time to read.

24. Look for activities offered in your community that don't cost any money such as concerts, demonstrations, or shows.

25. Leave your credit card at home when you go shopping. Using cold cash is less tempting than handing over a card.

Saving Money Now So You'll Have It Later

If you save only $5 per month at 5 percent interest that's compounded quarterly, here's what you'll have:

- ✧ After one year: $61.66
- ✧ After two years: $126.47
- ✧ After three years: $194.58
- ✧ After four years: $266.15
- ✧ After five years: $341.38
- ✧ After ten years: $779.04
- ✧ After fifteen years: $1,340.13

If you save $10 per month at 5 percent interest that's compounded quarterly, here's what you'll have:

- ✧ After one year: $123.29
- ✧ After two years: $252.86
- ✧ After three years: $382.03
- ✧ After four years: $532.13
- ✧ After five years: $682.53
- ✧ After ten years: $1,557.56
- ✧ After fifteen years: $2,679.38

If you save $15 per month at 5 percent interest that's compounded quarterly, here's what you'll have:

- ✧ After one year: $184.95
- ✧ After two years: $379.33
- ✧ After three years: $583.60
- ✧ After four years: $798.29
- ✧ After five years: $1,023.91
- ✧ After ten years: $2,336.60
- ✧ After fifteen years: $4,019.51

If you save $20 per month at 5 percent interest that's compounded quarterly, here's what you'll have:

- ✧ After one year: $249.58
- ✧ After two years: $505.71
- ✧ After three years: $778.03
- ✧ After four years: $1,064.27
- ✧ After five years: $1,365.06
- ✧ After ten years: $3,115.12
- ✧ After fifteen years: $5,358.76

Index

interest-bearing accounts,
159-160
Internet
purchasing on, 132
Teenagers Today Web site,
135
Yahoo car site, 149
Internet banks, 102-103
investing, 196-197
CDs, 200-203
IRAs, 203-204
money market accounts,
200-203
starting, 197-198
stock market, 204-207
investments, types, 199
IRAs (Individual Retirement
Accounts), 58, 69, 203-204

J–K

jobs
accident statistics, 59
choosing, 59-60
contacts, making, 63
creativity, 63
disparities, 59-60
learning from, 62
legal limits, age, 54-55
minimum wage, 56-58
obtaining, 54
physical labor, 60-62
prioritizing, 61

salary scales, 56-58
taxes, 58-59
joint checking accounts,
160-161

Keogh accounts, 69

L

Lavine, Alan, *Making Money
in Mutual Funds,* 202
leasing automobiles,
146-147
Lee Credit Unions, 102
lessons, learning,
allowances, 45-47
liabilities, 69
life insurance, loans, 71
lifeline checking accounts,
161
limited partnerships, 68
loans, 70

M

mail order shopping, 134
*Making Money in Mutual
Funds,* 202
minimum wage, 56-58
statistics, 57
money
choices, 22-23
happiness, 32-33
independence, 22

N

O

T